THE POWER OF TEAMWORK

MANAGING GENERATIONAL DIFFERENCES FOR A SAFER WORKPLACE

TONY N. MUDD

Copyright © 2024 by Tony N Mudd.

All rights reserved. NO part of this publication may be reproduced, stored in a retrieval system, transmitted in any form by any means of electronic, mechanical, photocopying, recording, or otherwise without written permission of the author or publisher, except by a reviewer who may quote brief passages in a review.

This author is represented by Mudd Family Publishing Company.

5011 Quail Court, Louisville, KY 40213

Email: muddfamilypub@gmail.com

ISBN: 9798320627786

Book Disclaimer

The information contained in this book is for general informational purposes only. It is not intended as a substitute for professional advice, guidance, or treatment. Before making any decisions based on the information provided, you should consult with qualified professionals who can assess your individual needs and circumstances.

The author and the publisher have made every effort to ensure that the information in this book is accurate and up to date at the time of publication. However, they make no representations or warranties of any kind, express or implied, about the completeness, accuracy, reliability, suitability, or availability of the information, products, services, or related graphics contained in this book. Any reliance you place on such information is strictly at your own risk.

In no event will the author or the publisher be liable for any loss or damage, including but not limited to indirect or consequential loss or damage, or any loss or damage whatsoever arising from the use of this book.

ABOUT THE AUTHOR

Tony Mudd, a EHS Culture Consultant, stands as a stalwart champion for workplace safety, driven by a deeply personal mission to ensure the safe return of every worker to their loved ones. This mission is deeply ingrained in his family history, sparked by the tragic workplace injury suffered by his grandfather—an event that profoundly altered the course of his family's life.

Armed with a Master's degree from Eastern Kentucky University, Tony embarked on a journey in Occupational Health and Safety spanning over a decade. His impactful work has left an indelible mark on the industrial Steel and Automotive manufacturing sectors, where he collaborated closely with Fortune 500 companies to minimize and eradicate recordable injuries.

Tony's tireless efforts not only saved companies substantial sums in worker compensation claims but also earned him esteemed recognition, including being honored in Louisville's 40 Under 40, receiving the National Safety Council's Rising Star Award, and securing a coveted spot as Linkedin's Top Safety Voice.

Tony's expertise extends beyond accolades. For a decade he has played a pivotal role in helping companies navigate the complexities of the modern age, fostering cohesive workplaces through his deep understanding of worker safety and team dynamics. As an accomplished author, Tony empowers leaders to effectively manage diverse workforces, advocating for collaboration and safety across all age groups.

Central to Tony's vision is the belief that technology holds the key to preventing workplace injuries and sparing families from enduring the trauma they entail.

Motivated by this conviction, he founded his own technology company dedicated to accident prevention through the meticulous analysis of safety data. Tony's unwavering dedication to making a lasting impact on worker safety is evident in his willingness to share his expertise through speaking engagements and engaging conversations about workplace safety in the modern age.

Table of Contents

Authors Dedication i

Acknowledgments...ii

Book Introduction iii

Chapter 1: Understanding Generational Dynamics in The Workplace..19

Chapter 2: Generational Differences on Safety Attitudes 39

Chapter 3: Using Mentorship Generational Collaboration..71

Chapter 4: Addressing Generational Differences in Safety Training…………………………………………..82

Chapter 5: Collaboration Among Leaders………....98

Chapter 6: Culture Among Generations...............123

Chapter 7: The Future of The Workplace…..........140

Authors Notes...124

DEDICATION

In honor of the workers who, in pursuit of their livelihoods, confronted unforeseen challenges and endured the aftermath of workplace accidents. This book serves as a testament to their resilience and a recognition of the profound impact on their lives and the lives of their families.

In loving memory of my grandfather, who tragically bore the burden of an injury sustained in the workplace. His experience stands as a poignant reminder of the imperative to tirelessly strive for a safer and more secure working environment for all.

To the families who have weathered the repercussions of workplace accidents, your courage and perseverance fuel the unwavering pursuit of creating a world where every worker returns home safely. This book is dedicated to those who have confronted adversity, both past and present, with the hope that our collective efforts will contribute to a future where workplace safety is paramount, and tragedies are minimized.

With profound respect,

Tony Mudd, CSP

ACKNOWLEDGMENTS

I extend my deepest gratitude to those whose unwavering support and collaboration have made the journey of writing this book a rewarding endeavor.

To my wife, your steadfast encouragement and understanding during late nights and early mornings fueled the creative process behind these pages. Your belief in this project was my constant motivation.

To my family, whose support has been a bedrock of strength throughout this endeavor. Your patience, encouragement, and shared enthusiasm have been invaluable.

To my friends, who offered a listening ear, words of encouragement, and occasional distractions that provided much-needed perspective during the writing process.

To my colleagues, whose insights, experiences, and shared passion for workplace safety have been instrumental in shaping the content of this book. Your dedication to preventing accidents has been both inspiring and instructive.

To the companies I've had the privilege of working with in the pursuit of accident prevention, thank you for opening your doors, sharing your experiences, and contributing to the collective knowledge that informs this work.

In recognition of the collaborative spirit that fuels the mission of creating safer workplaces, I express my deepest appreciation to each individual and entity that has played a part in bringing this book to fruition.

With sincere thanks,

Tony Mudd, CSP

INTRODUCTION

Dear reader, I want to personally thank you for investing your time in "The Power of Teamwork: Navigating Generational Differences for a Safer Workplace." In this book, I'll address some of the most challenging issues leaders face when managing multigenerational teams to prioritize and enhance worker safety.

This book serves as a roadmap for leaders like you, aiming to leverage the collective strengths of diverse age groups to ensure workplace safety. I firmly believe that we can all learn and grow together, but it requires understanding.

Understanding the dynamics of generational diversity is crucial in today's professional landscape. Through this book, you'll gain insights into how generational differences shape attitudes towards workplace safety, empowering management teams to tackle challenges in leading multigenerational teams.

We'll systematically explore common safety concerns among different generations, equipping you with the knowledge to tailor safety protocols effectively. Additionally, we'll investigate whether generational disparities influence responses to safety training, providing practical solutions to bridge potential gaps in compliance.

A key focus will be on communication strategies tailored to accommodate diverse generational preferences and learning styles. By leveraging technological advancements, you can effectively disseminate safety information, fostering a safety-centric culture resonating with employees across all age groups.

Moreover, I'll emphasize the importance of mentorship and cross-generational collaboration in enhancing safety initiatives. By nurturing collaborative relationships and tapping into the wisdom of experienced professionals, your organization can embed safety into every aspect of teamwork.

As workforce demographics evolve, I'll provide insights into anticipating and overcoming future challenges. By embracing proactive strategies and fostering continuous improvement, your organization can ensure that safety protocols evolve alongside the changing needs of the workforce.

Thank you again for joining me on this journey to create safer and more inclusive workplaces.

Warm regards,

Tony Mudd, CSP

CHAPTER 1: UNDERSTANDING GENERATIONAL DYNAMICS

"We have the power to make this the best generation of mankind in the history of the world or to make it the last." – **John F. Kennedy**

The pace of change in the workplace is relentless. Having spent over a decade as a Safety Professional, my journey has been about more than just preventing accidents. It's about navigating the complexities of teams, understanding varied communication styles, and ensuring safety resonates across all levels.

Today, our workplace landscape is markedly different. For the first time in history, we have five distinct generations coexisting under one roof: Traditionalists, Baby Boomers, Generation X, Millennials, and Generation Z. This convergence of generations brings unprecedented challenges for leaders like myself.

The dynamics of our workplace have evolved, and with it, the approach to safety. Leading teams in this modern era demands a keen awareness of these generational differences. It's about recognizing that each person has unique needs, motivations, and communication preferences.

As leaders, it's imperative that we adapt to this changing environment. We must stay attuned to the shifts and nuances, understanding how to effectively lead and inspire individuals across generations.

Recently, I had the opportunity to speak at the Future of EHS Technology conference in Louisville, KY. During the panel discussion, the moderator posed a thought-provoking question: how many generations currently comprise the workforce, and why is this significant?

In response, I offered an analogy: envision a group of individuals participating in a tug-of-war, each pulling the rope in a different direction with the singular aim of victory. However, due to their unique backgrounds, experiences, and biases, the rope eventually snaps, leaving everyone with a fragment in their grasp. The lesson? Success hinges on unity—a shared direction and mutual trust. But how can we achieve this when we lack familiarity with those beside us? This dilemma encapsulates the challenge leaders face—what I call the "*Five-Way Pull*" *of generational diversity.*

Indeed, these five generations—Traditionalists, Baby Boomers, Generation X, Millennials, and Generation Z—are all players in the game of tug-of-war within the workplace. Each group endeavors to lead, to be heard, accepted, and valued.

Consider the challenge of raising five children, each with vastly different views on life, wants, and needs. It's akin to walking a tightrope, striving to satisfy each one while maintaining harmony within the family unit.

Let's delve into the differences among these groups, as outlined in the Insight Global Report titled "Retaining a Multigenerational Workforce":

Traditionalists (The Silent Generation):

Born from 1922 to 1945, they comprise a mere 2 percent of the current workforce. Traditionalists prefer in-person or handwritten communication and value traits like dependability, straightforwardness, and loyalty. They uphold a worldview centered around hierarchy, obedience, and seniority, though many are now nearing the end of their careers.

Baby Boomers:

Born from 1946 to 1964, they make up roughly 25 percent of the workforce. Baby Boomers prefer efficient communication such as face-to-face interactions or phone calls. They are characterized as optimistic, team-oriented "workaholics" who prioritize making sacrifices for success and "paying one's dues."

Generation X:

Born from 1965 to 1980, they represent 33 percent of the current workforce. Generation Xers are known for their flexibility, informality, independence, and skepticism. They prioritize work-life balance and personal/professional interests over company interests, valuing diversity and acting swiftly if their needs aren't met.

Millennials:

Born from 1981 to 1996, they make up 35 percent of the workforce. Millennials are civic-minded, achievement-oriented individuals who seek challenge and growth. They prioritize purpose-driven work, work-life balance, and quality management, gravitating towards unique work experiences and opportunities for responsibility.

Generation Z:

Born from 1997 to the early 2010s, they currently represent 5 percent of the workforce and are rapidly growing. Generation Z is characterized as entrepreneurial, progressive, racially and ethnically diverse, and global-minded. They prefer innovative technologies, individualism, and prioritize diversity, personalization, and creativity over rigid structures.

Understanding these differences is crucial for leaders navigating the multigenerational workforce, enabling them to tailor their approach and foster a culture of inclusivity, collaboration, and mutual respect.

One of the most significant pitfalls I've observed in leaders striving to enhance worker safety within cross-generational teams is the tendency to prioritize making everyone happy and seeking unanimous agreement. However, there's a crucial distinction between accommodating diverse perspectives and simply aiming to please. Striving for consensus can lead to a culture of entitlement, where being heard becomes conflated with being spoiled.

Creating a positive workplace culture doesn't mean avoiding discomfort or conflict at all costs. It's about fostering an environment where individuals feel respected and valued, even amidst disagreements. We must recognize that genuine inclusivity entails more than just saying yes to everything—it involves embracing diverse viewpoints and engaging in constructive dialogue.

Reflecting on the film "Yes Man," starring Jim Carrey, we see the dangers of blindly agreeing to everything. While initially, the protagonist experiences a temporary boost in fortunes, he ultimately realizes that true fulfillment comes from being open to life's experiences and embracing authenticity. Similarly, leaders must prioritize authenticity and integrity over superficial consensus.

Another common mistake is the fear of saying the wrong thing and inadvertently causing offense. Whether it's mispronouncing names, overlooking someone's contributions, or expressing differing viewpoints, leaders may hesitate to speak out of fear of causing discomfort. However, genuine communication requires honesty and openness, even if it means navigating difficult conversations.

Ultimately, creating a vibrant and inclusive team environment requires leaders to strike a balance between accommodating diverse perspectives and upholding core values. It's about fostering an atmosphere where individuals feel empowered to voice their opinions, knowing that they will be heard and respected, even amidst disagreement. By prioritizing authenticity and open communication, leaders can navigate the complexities of cross-generational teams with confidence and integrity.

In the modern workplace, not only have individuals evolved, but so too has the very nature of conducting business. Consider the convenience of online shopping or the simplicity of ordering a pizza with a text message—these are just a few examples of how technology has transformed our daily lives. Similarly, in the workplace, we've witnessed a proliferation of tools and new technologies designed to enhance safety and efficiency.

From wearables that monitor vital signs to drones that survey hazardous areas, and from exoskeletons to virtual reality safety training programs, the array of innovations is staggering. The traditional reliance on paper has dwindled as digital solutions have become the norm. Employees are increasingly working remotely, transcending geographical boundaries, and entire industries are emerging to meet the demands of this evolving landscape.

Zoom and team meetings have replaced face-to-face interactions, while remote-controlled forklifts and virtual business operations enable companies to function seamlessly from the comfort of home. The modern workplace is a testament to the transformative power of technology, paving the way for unprecedented levels of connectivity, efficiency, and flexibility.

The dynamics of the workplace and business operations have undergone a profound transformation. As such, it is imperative that today's leaders adapt and evolve to meet the evolving needs and challenges of the modern world. One critical aspect of this evolution is the steadfast commitment to prioritizing safety and well-being in the workplace.

In today's rapidly changing landscape, where technology and innovation drive progress, leaders must remain vigilant in safeguarding the health and safety of their employees. Whether it's implementing cutting-edge safety protocols, staying abreast of emerging risks, or fostering a culture of accountability and care, leaders play a pivotal role in ensuring that safety remains paramount.

Moreover, as workplaces become increasingly interconnected and globalized, leaders must navigate new complexities and challenges. This includes addressing diverse workforce needs, embracing remote work arrangements, and leveraging technology to enhance safety practices.

By evolving with the times and prioritizing safety and well-being, today's leaders not only protect their employees but also foster a culture of trust, resilience, and innovation. In doing so, they lay the foundation for sustainable success in an ever-evolving landscape of work.

After conducting extensive research informed by my professional experience, one of the most frequently asked questions I encounter is: What is the most challenging issue in managing across generations? The primary hurdle lies in fostering meaningful connections. Despite the abundance of communication tools such as phones, email, and instant chat, many workplaces struggle to facilitate genuine connections during daily interactions and meetings, leading to a notable disconnect.

Consider this: individuals naturally gravitate towards those with whom they share common interests, inadvertently fostering separation and division within teams. Since the onset of COVID-19, the world has undergone a significant transformation in how we communicate and connect with one another. Gone are the days when physical presence was a necessity for meaningful interactions. Creating meaningful connections no longer requires leaving the comfort of one's home, room, or car.

Personally, I've been collaborating with individuals online for years, some of whom I've never had the opportunity to meet face-to-face. Employers face significant challenges ahead. To mitigate this issue, employers must take proactive steps:

Foster Connections:

Encourage informal gatherings: Organize regular team lunches, coffee breaks, or after-work social events where team members can interact in a relaxed setting. For example, hosting a monthly pizza lunch or a quarterly team outing to a local park or museum can provide opportunities for bonding outside of work tasks.

Facilitate team-building activities:

Plan team-building exercises that promote collaboration and trust among team members. This could include activities such as escape room challenges, outdoor adventure courses, or volunteer projects. For instance, organizing a team volunteer day at a local charity or organizing a friendly sports competition can foster teamwork and camaraderie.

Implement mentorship programs:

Pair employees from different generations as mentors and mentees to facilitate knowledge sharing and relationship-building. For example, mentees by Boomer employee could mentor a Millennial newcomer, providing guidance on navigating the industry, while the Millennial mentee could offer insights into emerging trends and technologies.

Tailored Communication:

It's essential to inquire about your team's communication preferences. Ask whether they prefer phone calls, text messages, chat platforms, or email for communication. Determine whether they favor virtual meetings or face-to-face interactions. Understand their learning style—do they prefer a lecture format or self-paced learning?

Additionally, inquire about their preferred mode of greeting, whether it's a handshake, a smile, or another gesture. Given the evolving nature of communication channels, addressing these preferences is crucial for effective collaboration.

Conduct communication preference surveys: Administer surveys or hold focus group discussions to help you better understand how to connect with your team.

Provide communication training:

Offer workshops or training sessions on effective communication skills tailored to different generations. For example, providing training on active listening techniques or email etiquette can help bridge communication gaps and promote understanding.

Utilize technology tools:

Implement multiple communication platforms that accommodate diverse preferences, such as Slack for instant messaging, Zoom for virtual meetings, or Trello for collaborative project management. By offering a range of communication tools, teams can choose the methods that best suit their individual needs and preferences.

Ensure Trustworthy Information:

This is a crucial point to consider, given the evolving nature of information consumption across generations. Just a couple of decades ago, individuals relied on traditional sources like morning news broadcasts, newspapers, or word-of-mouth to stay informed. However, in today's digital age, multiple generations turn to social media platforms such as Facebook, TikTok, or YouTube for news updates. While this instantaneous access to information offers undeniable benefits, it also presents potential challenges for organizations, particularly concerning topics like politics, regulatory compliance, or emerging trends.

We're currently immersed in an era of instant information, where individuals can pose a question to a computer and receive a response within milliseconds. This rapid exchange of information has accelerated the pace of change, sometimes at a rate that may feel overwhelming or difficult to keep up with. As a result, organizations must navigate this swiftly changing landscape with careful consideration and adaptability.

Establish a centralized communication hub:

Create a dedicated intranet portal or company website where employees can access reliable information about company updates, policies, and initiatives. Regularly update this platform with relevant news and announcements to keep everyone informed and aligned. It is also a good idea to create a social media policy outlining guidelines for social media usage in the workplace. This policy serves as a roadmap for team members, clarifying expectations and rationale behind the rules. This helps ensure that everyone is on the same page regarding how and where to find reliable information, fostering clarity and alignment across the team.

Designate communication ambassadors:

Appoint designated communication ambassadors within each team or department who are responsible for disseminating accurate information and addressing any questions or concerns. These ambassadors can serve as liaisons between leadership and team members, ensuring clear and consistent communication.

Encourage open dialogue:

Foster a culture of transparency and open communication where employees feel comfortable asking questions and sharing feedback. Hold regular town hall meetings, Q&A sessions, or feedback forums where leadership can address employee inquiries and provide updates on company initiatives. By promoting open dialogue, organizations can build trust and accountability among employees.

By implementing these strategies, organizations can foster stronger connections, improve communication, and enhance trust among team members across different generations. This, in turn, creates a more inclusive and cohesive workplace environment where employees feel valued and engaged.

As the workplace landscape continues to evolve, leaders may face challenges in attracting and recruiting younger generations, especially in the wake of the COVID-19 pandemic. Many individuals have become more entrepreneurial and are exploring opportunities to generate income online through platforms like YouTube, TikTok, or Etsy.

For instance, I recently heard from a colleague about a nurse friend who earns an additional $100,000 per year through side jobs and influencing on the internet. This showcases how younger generations are leveraging digital platforms to pursue alternative sources of income. They no longer feel as dependent on traditional employment and are less inclined to tolerate workplace dynamics or low wages.

Consider the appeal of creating viral content or selling handmade goods compared to working in conventional roles. The allure of instant success and personal fulfillment outweighs the monotony of assembly line work or navigating office politics for many individuals from younger generations. As a result, employers must adapt their recruitment strategies and workplace environments to remain attractive and competitive in this changing landscape.

For companies to thrive in this evolving landscape, they must embrace creativity and courage to differentiate themselves. Many companies have lost their internal entrepreneurial spirit, which is why I admire the startup environment where individuals are constantly innovating and driving change to propel the company forward.

In this dynamic environment, people are willing to take risks because they understand the potential rewards and opportunities for advancement. Personally, I believe that companies should explore initiatives like establishing internal investment groups to support employees' entrepreneurial endeavors. Offering loans or startup grants can empower employees to pursue their ideas and contribute to the company's growth in unexpected ways.

Moreover, I think companies often place too much emphasis on degree requirements for certain roles, overlooking individuals' ability to self-educate and acquire valuable skills. Consider a scenario where an employee aspires to work in marketing or sales but lacks a formal degree in the field. Despite their enthusiasm and dedication, they may feel constrained by educational barriers. However, their potential and commitment to self-improvement should not be underestimated.

Instead of solely focusing on academic credentials, companies should recognize and nurture the talents and ambitions of their employees. By providing opportunities for skill development, mentorship, and internal mobility, organizations can cultivate a culture of inclusivity and empower individuals to reach their full potential. Ultimately, investing in employees' growth and development benefits both the individual and the company, fostering a more engaged, motivated, and innovative workforce.

One prevalent issue I've noticed is the absence of clear career discovery paths within many companies. Employees often lack visibility into the trajectory of each role, regardless of its size or significance. To address this, companies should implement comprehensive career roadmaps for every position within their organization.

A career roadmap provides employees with a structured outline of potential career paths and advancement opportunities within the company. It offers insight into the skills, experiences, and milestones required to progress from one role to another, fostering a sense of direction and purpose among employees.

By establishing clear career pathways, companies empower employees to navigate their career journey with confidence. Employees can better understand how they can increase their earning potential, acquire new skills, and find greater satisfaction in their roles. Moreover, career roadmaps demonstrate the organization's commitment to employee development and growth, enhancing retention and engagement.

Ultimately, investing in career discovery initiatives and providing transparent career paths benefits both employees and the organization as a whole. It fosters a culture of continuous learning, professional advancement, and employee satisfaction, driving long-term success and prosperity.

When reflecting on these tools and strategies, I'm reminded of the numerous times I've had to pivot. Managing cross-generational teams demands dedication, effort, and a commitment to understanding and connecting with individuals who contribute daily to the company's success. Building these relationships takes time—a consideration often overlooked. Trust and comfort don't develop overnight; they require consistent effort and accountability to foster within the workplace.

Early indicators of ineffective leadership include team members seeking to depart. Therefore, it's imperative for modern leaders to continuously evolve and adapt to the changing times. This adaptability is crucial for maintaining a cohesive and engaged workforce.

As we conclude this chapter, it's clear that the landscape of information consumption and dynamics in the Workplace is rapidly evolving, with each generation adapting to new means of accessing and sharing knowledge. While the immediacy of digital platforms offers undeniable advantages, it also poses challenges for organizations striving to navigate complex issues in an era of rapid change.

In the next chapter, we'll delve deeper into the impact of generational differences on attitudes towards workplace safety. We'll explore how varying perspectives, values, and experiences shape individuals' perceptions of safety in the workplace. By understanding these dynamics, we can develop tailored strategies to promote a culture of safety that resonates across all generations.

CHAPTER 2: GENERATIONAL DIFFERENCES ON SAFETY ATTITUDES

"The greatest discovery of my generation is that a human being can alter his life by altering his attitudes." - **William James**

Last year, I had the privilege of sharing insights with the LinkedIn Top Experts online community, where the discussion revolved around the profound impact of generational differences on attitudes towards workplace safety. This topic holds immense significance in understanding the evolving nature of the modern workplace and its inherent challenges.

Generational disparities significantly influence individuals' perceptions of workplace safety. Reflecting on this, I recall the tragic experience of my grandfather, a dedicated veteran of 30 years in his industry. On January 24, 1996, tragedy struck when Joe, a seasoned professional and devoted husband and father, headed to work and never returned home.

That fateful night, Joe's wife received a distressing call urging her to rush to the jobsite. Upon arrival, she was met with a scene of chaos and anguish, where she learned that Joe had been crushed by 5,000 pounds of lumber, a consequence of an oversight by an untrained crane operator. Despite surviving the incident physically, Joe's life was forever altered, as he endured months of reconstructive surgery and grueling rehabilitation.

As Joe's grandson, I witnessed firsthand the profound impact of this ordeal on his life. From grappling with physical limitations to enduring the emotional toll of post-traumatic stress disorder, Joe's once vibrant spirit was irrevocably changed. This harrowing experience transformed his outlook on safety, instilling a heightened sense of caution and skepticism towards unfamiliar practices or technologies.

It's important to note that Joe's altered perspective on safety was not solely dictated by his age or gender, but rather by his personal encounter with trauma and suffering. This poignant lesson underscores the profound influence of individual experiences on attitudes towards workplace safety and emphasizes the need for empathy and understanding in fostering a culture of safety and well-being.

On the other hand, as a millennial, I prioritize purpose, diversity, and technological advancements in my approach to workplace safety. Embracing change as an opportunity, I recognize the value of innovation and proactive measures in ensuring a safe work environment. Contrasting with my grandfather's hands-on and mechanical approach, characterized by a macho perspective on safety, I prioritize caution and avoidance of potential hazards.

Reflecting on my grandfather's dedication and sacrifice for his family, I'm reminded of the future that was unjustly taken from him. His experience profoundly shaped my beliefs and attitudes towards safety, serving as a poignant reminder of the importance of prioritizing well-being above all else.

For me, it's not merely a matter of generational differences, but rather the individual experiences that shape our perspectives on safety. As a new graduate in the field of Occupational Safety, I often heard warnings about the risks associated with veteran employees' overconfidence and complacency. While there may be some truth to this, I believe that complacency knows no age, gender, or body type. Whether driving a car, riding a bike, or simply navigating stairs, we all have the potential to become complacent and overlook safety protocols, putting ourselves and others at risk. Thus, it's imperative for everyone, regardless of age or experience, to remain vigilant and proactive in ensuring safety in every aspect of our lives.

When leading cross-generational teams, it's imperative to recognize the unique perspectives, preferences, and communication styles of each generation while ensuring that safety standards remain consistent across the board. This becomes particularly crucial in today's diverse workforce landscape, where different generations bring varying experiences, attitudes, and approaches to workplace safety.

Earlier this year, I had the privilege of engaging with an MBA student from Cranfield University in the UK, who was exploring avenues to enhance employee engagement, with a specific focus on workplace safety initiatives spanning different generations. This inquiry prompted a reflection on my extensive experience as an Industrial Safety Professional within the Steel and Automotive manufacturing sectors, where I've witnessed firsthand the challenges and opportunities associated with fostering effective safety engagement across diverse age groups.

In response to these challenges, I developed and implemented a comprehensive three-step approach aimed at promoting safety engagement within a manufacturing company. Over the course of 12 months, we embarked on an internal safety engagement program that leveraged a combination of multimedia platforms and communication channels to effectively reach and resonate with employees at all levels.

One integral aspect of our strategy involved the daily dissemination of workplace safety fail videos, strategically showcased on canteen and laptop monitors. These videos served as tangible reminders of potential hazards and safety protocols, sparking discussions and raising awareness among employees. Complementing this visual component, we introduced a series of intriguing safety quotes, strategically shared through email, Teams chat, and text notifications throughout the workday. These bite-sized insights not only reinforced safety messaging but also encouraged reflection and dialogue among team members.

Furthermore, we recognized the importance of fostering a sense of community and inclusivity in our safety engagement efforts. To achieve this, we established a bi-weekly safety newsletter, meticulously curated to cover a wide range of safety topics, updates, and recognition initiatives. Importantly, this newsletter wasn't limited to employees; it was also extended to their families, underscoring our commitment to transparency and accountability in safety practices.

The implementation of these multifaceted strategies yielded tangible results, fostering a culture of safety engagement and collaboration within the organization. Employees from different generations began to actively engage in safety conversations, sharing insights, concerns, and best practices. The lunchroom became a hub of discussion, as colleagues exchanged experiences and learned from one another's perspectives.

Notably, the success of our approach transcended organizational boundaries, prompting its adoption in a sister facility. This scalability underscored the efficacy of our strategies in fostering meaningful engagement and driving positive safety outcomes across diverse contexts.

In essence, our experience exemplifies the transformative power of tailored, creative, and cost-effective safety engagement initiatives. By acknowledging and embracing the unique characteristics and preferences of each generation, organizations can cultivate a culture of safety that resonates with employees at all levels. As employers, it's incumbent upon us to invest in initiatives that foster community, communication, and collaboration around safety, ultimately ensuring the well-being and productivity of our workforce.

Engagement is rooted in meaningful conversation, shared experiences, and mutual interests. When it comes to sparking conversation and capturing attention, safety is a topic that universally resonates with people. Think about it - why do we gravitate towards news articles or broadcasts about safety-related issues, whether it's health concerns, financial security, or personal well-being? It's because safety matters to everyone, and it's inherently compelling.

Yet, despite the undeniable importance of safety, many organizations overlook the power of engaging their workforce on this critical topic. While they invest significant resources in external social media campaigns, internal safety initiatives often receive minimal attention and funding.

But here's the thing: your employees, your team members, they're just as vital as your external customers. Some even refer to them as internal customers because their well-being directly impacts on your organization's success. That's why it's crucial to cultivate an internal following around safety, akin to the dynamics of social media platforms.

Imagine creating a space where your team can share insights, exchange ideas, and actively participate in safety-related discussions. By fostering this internal community focused on safety, you not only promote awareness and vigilance but also empower your team to take ownership of their well-being. It's an investment in your most valuable asset - your people - and it's one that yields invaluable returns in terms of safety culture and organizational success.

As a seasoned professional who has worked in numerous organizations, I've witnessed a wide spectrum of workplace environments. From bustling and vibrant atmospheres to disheartening scenes where employees felt neglected and unheard. One particular experience that stands out occurred during my tenure with a large paint manufacturing company in Louisville, KY.

Excited to contribute positively to the team upon being hired, I was greeted with an unexpected turn of events on my first day. Driving into the plant, I was met with a sight I had never encountered before

- employees on strike, expressing their frustration and discontent. The atmosphere inside the plant mirrored this unrest, with a sense of defeat lingering in the air.

In that same week, the plant faced additional challenges including a fire and a roof collapse, exacerbating the sense of neglect and disconnection among the workforce. Their concerns about safety fell on deaf ears, leaving them feeling abandoned and disregarded.

However, I've also had the privilege of working in organizations with robust safety cultures where employees felt valued, protected, and integral to the company's success. These experiences taught me the importance of organizational readiness for change and the pivotal role of leadership in fostering receptivity and optimism.

In essence, my journey through various workplace environments has underscored the critical importance of listening to employees, fostering a culture of inclusion and engagement, and being prepared to adapt and evolve in response to challenges and opportunities.

In my experience, leaders can take several steps to enhance safety engagement across different generations, fostering a more inclusive working environment. These strategies include:

Understanding Generational Perspectives:

Conduct surveys or focus groups to gather insights into the safety attitudes and preferences of different generations within your workforce. For instance, Baby Boomers may prioritize traditional safety protocols and face-to-face communication, while Millennials and Generation Z may prefer technology-driven solutions like Virtual Reality (VR) training.

Foster intergenerational discussions where employees can freely share their safety perspectives without fear of judgment. This might involve hosting panel discussions or workshops where representatives from each generation share their experiences and concerns regarding workplace safety.

Adapting Safety Policies and Procedures:

Review safety policies and procedures to ensure they cater to the preferences and needs of all generations. Consider offering flexible work arrangements to accommodate employees with physical limitations or health concerns, while also providing remote training options for those who prefer digital learning.

Integrate technology-driven safety solutions, such as mobile apps for hazard reporting or wearable devices for health tracking, to appeal to tech-savvy generations while ensuring accessibility for those less familiar with new technologies.

Leading by Example:

Senior leaders should visibly demonstrate their commitment to safety by adhering to established protocols and wearing personal protective equipment (PPE) in all work areas. This conveys a message of accountability and underscores the importance of safety for employees of all ages.

Encourage all leaders to conduct regular safety inspections and audits, showcasing their proactive approach to hazard identification and mitigation. Consistently prioritizing safety in actions and decisions sets a positive example for employees at every level.

Providing Feedback and Recognition:

Implement a safety recognition program to acknowledge individuals or teams for their contributions to workplace safety. This could include monthly safety awards, peer-to-peer recognition, or public acknowledgment during team meetings.

Encourage employees to offer feedback on safety initiatives and policies, and actively listen to their suggestions for improvement. Regular safety feedback sessions provide a platform for employees to voice concerns and contribute ideas for enhancing safety measures.

Foster a Culture of Psychologically Safety:

Encourage all generations in the workplace to embrace a culture of giving and receiving feedback respectfully. Create a safe space where employees feel empowered to share their thoughts, ideas, and concerns without fear of judgment or repercussion. Encourage constructive feedback by focusing on specific behaviors or actions rather than personal characteristics.

Emphasize the importance of active listening and empathy in understanding diverse perspectives. By promoting a culture of respectful feedback, you can enhance psychological safety across all generations, fostering open communication, collaboration, and mutual respect in the workplace.

Incorporating these strategies into your leadership approach can effectively bridge generational gaps and foster a culture of safety across diverse teams.

One of the most daunting challenges faced by management teams when leading modern multi-generational teams is fostering communication among team members. Consider the countless times you've stepped into an elevator and noticed everyone avoiding eye contact, or how strangers instinctively avert their gaze when passing each other to avoid interaction and maintain solitude.

I've heard that some international and foreign companies tackle this issue by organizing workplace social events, such as mixers with refreshments before meetings. They even go as far as hosting fun compctitions where employees can watch their CEO dance, creating a lighthearted atmosphere conducive to connecting with others. However, this approach seems rare in American companies where the norm is often a rush from one meeting to only be late to the next.

If we aim to effectively manage the new-age workforce, we must embrace innovative approaches. For instance, periodically changing up meeting spaces can offer a refreshing backdrop for multi-generational teams. Picture a company meeting held at a movie theater, where team members can enjoy popcorn, purchase drinks, and relax in comfortable chairs while conducting business. I've even heard of companies revolutionizing their hiring process by incorporating live escape room games to assess a candidate's qualities as a team player, empathy, active listening skills, helpfulness, and positive attitude. Implementing such initiatives requires courage to break away from traditional norms and lead teams like never before.

For modern management groups tasked with leading multigenerational teams, it's crucial to introspect and confront our own misconceptions, stereotypes, and biases. Through my experiences collaborating with various teams, I've encountered pervasive misunderstandings and preconceptions surrounding the leadership of multigenerational groups. Addressing these challenges head-on is imperative for leaders who are shaping the future of the workplace and striving to cultivate a more inclusive and equitable work environment.

Here are some prevalent myths to contemplate when managing new-age teams. Let's delve into them.

Myth Number 1: Baby boomers are resistant to adopting new technology. This assumption couldn't be further from the truth.

As AI continues to revolutionize industries, the old adage "you can't teach an old dog new tricks" resurfaces, but it's a misleading notion. Across various sectors and generations, workers are actively embracing new skills as jobs evolve with digitization and automation. While exceptions may exist, this trend is evident across the board.

Interestingly, assumptions about technological prowess extend beyond older workers. Contrary to popular belief, evidence suggests that Gen Z isn't universally adept with workplace technology. (Pickup & Anekola, 2023). Honestly, the younger generation excels in using social media technologies like Instagram, Snapchat, and others. However, there's a notable difference when it comes to workplace technologies such as Microsoft products like Outlook, Excel, PowerPoint, Power BI, or Google Suite products like Google Sheets or Slides. Conversely, older generations often demonstrate proficiency in workplace tech and exhibit eagerness to expand their knowledge.

Let's consider my 72-year-old mother-in-law as a prime example. With a distinguished career spanning 30 years as a budget analyst for the United States Army, she has honed her technological skills to an impressive degree. Proficient in Microsoft Excel for creating intricate spreadsheets and PowerPoint for delivering polished presentations, she seamlessly integrates technology into her daily tasks. From crafting detailed financial reports to designing captivating graphs, she adeptly utilizes email, text messaging, and video conferencing tools. Despite belonging to an older generation, she effortlessly navigates a wide array of technological platforms and applications.

Remarkably, she remains actively engaged on social media platforms like Facebook, leveraging the internet for online shopping and staying connected with relatives. What's more, she can outpace even me, a millennial, in sending text messages. It's evident that she not only embraces technology but also derives genuine enjoyment from utilizing it to its fullest extent. Now, consider this: how many of us have truly mastered technology that has been around for ages? It's a question worth pondering. Often, when I attend meetings, I encounter individuals from my own generation who struggle with basic tasks such as creating spreadsheets, generating charts with Power BI, or, at worst, designing presentations that are both visually appealing and engaging enough to keep the audience awake.

By perpetuating this myth, employers may inadvertently stifle progress. According to the latest skills report, nearly half of all surveyed individuals reported feeling disengaged at work due to a lack of skills development and training opportunities. (Callahan & Callahan, 2023) Both Baby Boomers and Gen X actively seek avenues for skill enhancement.

Myth Number 2: Gen Z are tech wizards, the know-how generation.

One of the prevailing misconceptions is that Generation Z, or Gen Z, is naturally skilled with technology. However, recent reports suggest otherwise. Contrary to popular belief, Gen Z isn't universally tech-savvy, especially in the workplace.

It turns out that Gen Zers harbor a common secret: they're not as adept with new technology as older generations presume. While they may have grown up in a digital age with immediate access to information and a penchant for digital devices, this doesn't necessarily translate into innate tech proficiency, particularly in professional settings.

New research reveals that many young professionals experience "tech shame" due to this assumption from older generations. According to a news article called "Quiet quitters, snowflakes: Debunking generational stereotypes in the workplace", one in five of the 18-to-29-year-olds polled felt judged when encountering technical issues, compared to only one in 25 for those aged 40 years and over. Additionally, 25% of the former age group would actively avoid participating in a meeting if they anticipated their tech tools causing disruption, whereas it was just 6% for the latter cohort.

Meanwhile, older generations demonstrate a keen aptitude for workplace technology and are often eager to expand their knowledge further, dispelling the notion that Gen Zer's inherently excel in this realm. Employers who have embraced this myth may inadvertently exacerbate workplace anxiety and create unforeseen challenges.

Myth Number 3: Gen Z and Millennials are lazy and don't care about work.

Gen Zers have distinguished themselves with the "quiet quitting" movement, often leaving the office promptly at or before 5 p.m. and emphasizing a strict work-life balance. However, it was the millennials who initially challenged traditional working conditions accepted by preceding generations. Callahan and Callahan (2023)

Today, there's a prevalent misconception that these two younger demographics lack commitment to work and are inherently lazy. Yet, the reality is quite different—they prioritize flexibility and seek employment with organizations that share their values and ideals.

When reflecting on the myth, I can't help but consider my own journey as a 34-year-old millennial who has been working since the age of 16. Throughout my life, I've held over 50 different jobs. But why so many? It's because, for a significant portion of my career, I was unsure about my future path. Many of the jobs I took lacked opportunities for growth, offered inadequate wages, and lacked diversity in the workplace. Out of those fifty jobs, only one or two were truly fulfilling and aligned with my aspirations.

I didn't just want a job; I yearned for a meaningful career—one that would allow me to make a difference and resonate with my identity. But finding that career path wasn't easy. It required a considerable amount of self-discovery and introspection. I put in long hours, often working 50 to 60 hours per week, in pursuit of that elusive career that would bring me fulfillment and purpose.

According to Deloitte's 2023 Gen Z and Millennials survey, 62% of millennials and 49% of Gen Z individuals perceive their work as being as important as, if not more important than, activities like exercise, music, or hobbies—ranking second only to family and friends.

Millennials are renowned for their strong work ethic, yet they also value the integration of work and personal life, which allows them to work more efficiently and effectively. Unlike the traditional "head-down" approach to work, millennials prioritize achieving a healthy work-life balance, enabling them to maintain productivity without sacrificing their well-being.

Moreover, both millennials and Gen Z are increasingly unwilling to tolerate jobs that endanger their health or well-being. Personally, I reflect on the experiences of my own family members, such as my mother, who worked as a Medical Assistant for over 30 years. Her dedication ended abruptly after an on-the-job injury, which not only deprived her of acknowledgment and compensation but also forced her into early retirement.

Similarly, my grandfather suffered a workplace injury and was promptly terminated once he could no longer fulfill his duties. These experiences illuminated the harsh reality of corporate loyalty: it's often a one-sided expectation, only reciprocated if one ascends to a leadership position within the organization.

In reality, millennials are thriving in what I term a "hustle culture" grinding 25/8 on social media platforms. Many of them juggle multiple jobs while managing a side business, caring for their families, or maintaining a household. It's not uncommon to find millennials also providing care for ill or dependent parents who can no longer work. In their relentless pursuit of goals, many millennials sacrifice sleep, constantly striving to stay motivated and fulfill their responsibilities, particularly those who work remotely and find themselves working around the clock without clear boundaries between work and personal time.

When considering Gen Z, it's crucial to recognize that they are often unfairly judged and misunderstood. Many of them came of age during the challenging times of the COVID-19 pandemic, experiencing a world that had abruptly shut down around them. They missed out on crucial human connections and the opportunity to cultivate meaningful experiences and relationships. Instead, they found themselves attending school online, navigating socially distanced proms, and graduating in unconventional settings such as their own front yards.

Growing up behind screens, Gen Z has nevertheless demonstrated remarkable qualities. They possess a unique sense of style, a natural curiosity, and a willingness to challenge traditions. Despite facing adversity, they show ingenuity and resourcefulness, often venturing into entrepreneurship with minimal support or resources. Their creativity knows no bounds.

It's essential to resist the temptation to label Gen Z as spoiled or privileged. Every generation faces its own set of challenges and advantages, and it's through embracing change and fostering understanding that progress is made. Instead of looking down on the next generation, we should acknowledge their strengths and contributions, recognizing that their unique perspective and experiences will shape the future in meaningful ways.

Stereotypes and misconceptions serve no real purpose. They attempt to categorize individuals into neat boxes, simplifying the complexity of human beings. The truth is, each person is unique and multifaceted, defying simplistic labels or generalizations. We are intricate creatures, shaped by our experiences, beliefs, and backgrounds.

It's essential to tread carefully around stereotypes and misconceptions because they can lead to harmful outcomes. Throughout history, many atrocities have occurred due to the misunderstanding and misrepresentation of entire groups of people. When we stop communicating, listening, and trying to understand each other, trust erodes, and divisions deepen.

To create a better future, we must strive to become better individuals. We need to reject stereotypes and misconceptions, instead embracing diversity, empathy, and understanding. By learning from the mistakes of the past and fostering genuine connections with one another, we can build a more inclusive and compassionate world.

For organizations to overcome workplace divisions stemming from generational stereotypes and cliques, organizations can implement the following strategies:

Offer Skills Development:

To offer skills development for cross-generational groups, organizations can implement various strategies aimed at enhancing collaboration and teamwork among employees from different age groups. One effective approach is to provide comprehensive training programs that focus on essential skills such as effective communication, conflict resolution, and cultural competence. These programs can be tailored to address the diverse needs and preferences of employees across different generations.

Effective communication training can help employees learn how to communicate more clearly and respectfully with colleagues of all ages, fostering better understanding and cooperation within teams. Conflict resolution training equips employees with the skills to manage disagreements and resolve conflicts constructively, promoting a more harmonious work environment. Additionally, cultural competence training enables employees to appreciate and respect the cultural differences among team members, leading to more inclusive and collaborative interactions.

For instance, let's consider a large multinational corporation with a diverse workforce spanning multiple generations, including Baby Boomers, Gen X, Millennials, and Gen Z. The company recognizes the importance of fostering collaboration and teamwork across these generational divides to maximize productivity and innovation.

To address this, the organization implements a series of skills development workshops focused on enhancing intergenerational communication and teamwork. One such workshop is titled "*Effective Communication Across Generations.*" During the workshop, employees from different age groups participate in interactive sessions led by experienced facilitators. They engage in role-playing exercises, group discussions, and case studies designed to explore communication challenges and opportunities across generations.

For example, participants may role-play common workplace scenarios where generational differences in communication styles and preferences become apparent. They discuss how different generations prefer to receive feedback, share ideas, and collaborate on projects.

Additionally, the workshop covers strategies for bridging these communication gaps, such as active listening techniques, adapting communication styles to suit different preferences, and leveraging technology to facilitate cross-generational collaboration.

By the end of the workshop, participants gain a deeper understanding of each other's communication styles, preferences, and perspectives. They also acquire practical skills and strategies to communicate more effectively across generational boundaries, fostering stronger relationships and teamwork within the organization.

By offering these training programs, organizations can create a supportive learning environment where employees from different generations can enhance their skills together, ultimately contributing to a more cohesive and productive workforce."

Implement Training to Discourage Negative Stereotypes:

To address negative stereotypes and biases in the workplace, it's important to begin by educating employees about their harmful effects. This can be achieved through training sessions or workshops that shed light on how stereotypes impact individuals, teams, and the overall work environment. Emphasizing the value of diversity and inclusion is essential in fostering a more inclusive workplace culture. Encouraging open discussions about different perspectives, experiences, and backgrounds helps employees recognize the benefits of a diverse workforce in driving innovation and creativity.

Furthermore, employees should be encouraged to question their own assumptions and beliefs about different generations. Providing examples of common stereotypes and prompting participants to reflect on their accuracy and validity fosters critical thinking and open-mindedness. Tailored training programs should be implemented to bridge generational gaps and promote understanding among employees of different age groups. These programs should focus on developing empathy, communication skills, and appreciation for diverse viewpoints.

Additionally, offering opportunities for skills development plays a crucial role in promoting collaboration and teamwork across generations. Training in areas such as effective communication, conflict resolution, and cultural competence equips employees with the tools needed to navigate intergenerational dynamics effectively. By implementing these initiatives, organizations can create a more inclusive and harmonious work environment where employees of all generations feel valued and respected.

Empower Younger Team Members:

Empower younger employees by giving them opportunities to contribute their unique perspectives and ideas. Encourage them to take on leadership roles and participate in decision-making processes.

The idea of using a large dry erase board to address company challenges is an excellent example of engaging younger generations in problem-solving and fostering innovation within the workplace. During my time working with a plant manager at a manufacturing company, I witnessed firsthand how this approach encouraged active participation and creativity among younger team members.

The manager would regularly write down company challenges on the board and invite team members to brainstorm solutions during designated times throughout the day. This practice created an open forum where individuals felt empowered to contribute their ideas without fear of judgment. There were no right or wrong answers, only opportunities to think critically and propose innovative solutions.

I observed that many younger employees gravitated towards the dry erase board, eagerly brainstorming ideas and collaborating with their peers. They approached challenges with enthusiasm and determination, often dedicating time outside of scheduled meetings to refine their solutions. While not every idea proved successful, each contribution was valued and served as a steppingstone towards finding effective solutions.

This practice not only empowered younger team members to take ownership of problem-solving but also allowed the organization to tap into their fresh perspectives and creative thinking. By involving younger generations in such initiatives, organizations can harness the full potential of their workforce and drive innovation and success.

Establish a Feedback System:

Create a feedback mechanism where employees can share their experiences and suggestions for improving communication and collaboration across generations. Use this feedback to develop strategies and initiatives that promote better interaction and understanding among employees of different age groups.

Take this scenario into consideration: Let's consider a mid-sized software development company that is looking to improve communication and collaboration among its cross-generational teams. To address this, the company has decided to implement a feedback system called "Open Door Fridays."

Every Friday afternoon, from 2:00 PM to 4:00 PM, the company designates a conference room as the "Open Door Room." During this time, employees from all departments and hierarchical levels are encouraged to drop in and provide feedback, share ideas, or raise concerns directly with senior management, including the CEO.

To facilitate the process, the company appoints a rotating team of facilitators from different departments who are responsible for managing the sessions and documenting feedback. These facilitators are trained to ensure that everyone has an opportunity to speak, and discussions remain constructive and respectful.

Employees are encouraged to offer feedback on various aspects of the company, such as work processes, team dynamics, company culture, and even suggestions for improvement. They can also share success stories, recognize their colleagues' achievements, and propose innovative ideas.

To encourage participation, the company provides incentives such as recognition awards, small tokens of appreciation, or opportunities for professional development for employees who actively engage in the feedback sessions.

Following each session, the feedback is compiled, analyzed, and shared with the relevant departments or teams for further discussion and action. Senior management takes proactive steps to address any issues raised, implement suggested improvements, or provide updates on the progress of previous feedback items.

Over time, "Open Door Fridays" have become an integral part of the company culture, fostering transparency, trust, and collaboration across generational divides. Employees feel valued and empowered, knowing that their voices are heard, and their feedback contributes to positive change within the organization.

By implementing these strategies, organizations can break down generational barriers and create a more cohesive and inclusive workplace culture where employees of all ages feel valued and respected.

In today's dynamic landscape, organizations must exhibit unparalleled flexibility to assemble and retain top-tier teams. We inhabit a world where potential employees can submit job applications in less than 60 seconds, thanks to the abundance of job boards and postings. While governmental initiatives aimed at creating more job opportunities may benefit job seekers, they can pose challenges for businesses striving to maintain their competitive edge. That's why it is crucial for companies to transition towards a more inclusive and diverse culture that caters to the needs and strengths of all generations.

CHAPTER 3: MENTORSHIP GENERATIONAL COLLABORATION

"We must find time to stop and thank those people who make a difference in our lives." - **JFK**

In order to progress and innovate, it's imperative that we leverage the collective knowledge, experiences, and perspectives of individuals across generations. This rings particularly true as we navigate the evolving landscape of workplace safety. Intergenerational collaboration stands as a cornerstone for fostering a culture of safety and continuous improvement.

It involves bringing together people from diverse backgrounds and age groups, allowing them to engage in open dialogue, share their expertise, and collectively work towards creating safer work environments. In this collaborative spirit, each individual contributes uniquely, recognizing that no one person holds superiority over another.

I once read a story about two unlikely creatures a Nile Crocodile and Egyptian plover bird. Imagine a sprawling riverbank teeming with life, where the mighty Nile Crocodile and the diminutive Egyptian plover bird form an unlikely but remarkable partnership. Picture the crocodile, with its powerful jaws and menacing presence, resting lazily on the riverbank, while the plover bird flits about nearby, chirping cheerfully.

In this curious dance of nature, the crocodile opens its massive jaws, revealing rows of sharp teeth gleaming in the sunlight. It's an intimidating sight, yet the plover bird shows no fear. With precise agility, it swoops in, darting between the crocodile's teeth like a skilled acrobat navigating a treacherous obstacle course.

As the bird meticulously pecks away at the tiny bits of meat lodged between the crocodile's teeth, it's not merely performing a chore; it's engaging in a vital act of mutualism. The crocodile, in its lumbering might, relies on the plover bird to keep its mouth clean and free from infection. In return, the plover bird benefits from a steady food source and protection from predators, as it flits fearlessly around the crocodile's formidable form.

In this symbiotic relationship, the giant reptile and the tiny bird are interconnected in a delicate balance of dependence and reciprocity. Each relies on the other for survival, forming an inseparable bond forged by the rhythms of nature. Just as the crocodile provides a haven for the plover bird, the plover bird fulfills an essential role in the crocodile's ecosystem, illustrating the profound interconnectedness of all living beings.

As we reflect on this extraordinary tale from the natural world, we're reminded of the power of collaboration and mutual support. Like the crocodile and the plover bird, seemingly disparate individuals and groups can come together, each contributing their unique strengths and abilities to achieve a common goal. In embracing our interdependence and recognizing the value of cooperation, we can forge stronger, more resilient communities and ecosystems, where every member thrives in harmony with the whole.

In the natural world, such mutualistic relationships are referred to as ecological interactions, where two or more species depend on each other for their social well-being. These symbiotic connections are abundant throughout nature, yet it's intriguing that the most intelligent and gifted creatures such as humans often struggle with the basics, such as sharing or cooperating for mutual benefit. It prompts us to question if we are the creature's beings on Earth. However, the more pressing question is how—how do these alliances form? How do different species recognize the need to collaborate and realize that they need each other?

It is my speculation that mutualistic relationships often originate from necessity and evolution. Consider some of the most significant partnerships in history—they often stem from fundamental needs: the need to eat, to procreate, to survive. Species realize that there is someone who can assist them, and they are willing to reciprocate.

Take, for instance, the partnership between Steve Jobs and Steve Wozniak. With Wozniak's technological expertise (he designed and built the first Apple computer) complementing Jobs' marketing prowess, this duo became titans of the digital world. Despite their tumultuous relationship and Wozniak's departure from Apple in 1985, their collaborative efforts paved the way for intuitive devices like iPhones and iPads that we rely on today.

Another remarkable partnership is exemplified by Helen Keller and Anne Sullivan. In 1887, at just 20 years old, Anne Sullivan embarked on a mission to teach Helen Keller, who was deaf, blind, and mute, to communicate effectively. Despite Sullivan's own partial blindness, she employed innovative techniques to teach Keller braille, multiplication tables, and sign language within months. Keller went on to become the first deaf-blind person to graduate from college in the United States.

Consider also the partnership between William Procter and James Gamble, who would go on to establish one of the world's largest companies. Procter, a candle maker, was married to Olivia Norris, while Gamble, a soap maker, was married to Olivia's sister Elizabeth. Encouraged by their father-in-law, who recognized that they were competing for the same raw materials, they merged their candle and soap-making operations in 1837 to create Procter & Gamble.

Today, P&G is a multinational consumer goods company with over 100 thousand employees and a market capitalization exceeding $200 billion. Some of its most successful brands include Crest, Charmin, Gillette, and Head & Shoulders. It's remarkable to think that such a behemoth corporation began with a simple suggestion from a father-in-law.

Recently, while writing a blog on Medium, I was approached by a Community Development Specialist from a Human Resource organization seeking advice on how to establish mentorship programs and foster cross-generational collaboration to enhance workplace dynamics. I emphasized to them that such initiatives could yield significant benefits, not only improving workplace safety but also fostering stronger connections among team members and enhancing accountability among management.

The essence of mentorship and collaboration across generations lies in the convergence of different perspectives and levels of expertise, united by a common goal to achieve positive outcomes, which is essential for thriving businesses. By pairing individuals with varying experiences and understanding, these programs create opportunities for mutual learning and growth.

However, the true value of such initiatives is realized through the cultivation of relationships across generations. Building stronger connections enables individuals to engage in meaningful conversations beyond formal meetings, fostering an environment were seeking guidance and asking questions becomes second nature.

To effectively implement these programs, employers must consider several key factors:

Start with the Safety Committee or Safety Teams:

Initiating mentorship and cross-generational collaboration within existing safety committees or teams can be advantageous. These groups often already exhibit a commitment to the organization's mission and safety goals. Engaging them in mentorship programs can reinforce their dedication to workplace safety while fostering intergenerational connections.

Choose Individuals Willing to Participate:

Selecting volunteers who are eager to engage in the program is crucial. Look for individuals within the organization who demonstrate enthusiasm for learning and connecting with colleagues from different generations. Their willingness to participate ensures active engagement and fosters a positive mentorship experience.

Select Individuals with a Positive Attitude:

Look for individuals who possess a positive attitude toward learning and collaboration. A constructive mindset encourages open communication and receptiveness to new ideas, facilitating meaningful interactions between mentors and mentees. Positive attitudes contribute to a supportive and conducive mentorship environment.

Ensure Availability of Participants:

Prioritize individuals who can commit time and effort to the mentorship program. Effective mentorship requires regular communication and engagement, so it's essential to choose participants who are available and willing to invest in the relationship. Availability fosters consistent interaction and facilitates knowledge sharing between mentors and mentees.

Establish Clear Expectations and Guidelines:

Define clear expectations and guidelines for participants to ensure a structured and productive mentorship experience. Develop a roadmap outlining the objectives, responsibilities, and communication protocols for both mentors and mentees. This roadmap can include discussion topics, team-building activities, and problem-solving exercises tailored to leverage the diverse knowledge and experiences of participants. Clear guidelines help maintain focus and alignment throughout the mentorship journey, maximizing its effectiveness in enhancing workplace safety and collaboration.

Picture this scenario: a prominent Manufacturing Company, a medium-sized firm renowned for its expertise in automotive parts, has launched a mentorship program with a singular goal in mind – to bolster workplace safety through cross-generational collaboration. As part of this initiative, the company has meticulously paired ten mentors with mentees drawn from various departments and spanning different age groups.

For instance, John, a seasoned machine operator in his late 50s, serves as a mentor to Sarah, a recent graduate in her early 20s working as a junior technician. Their collaboration begins with an orientation session where they establish mutual goals, focusing on improving safety awareness and identifying workplace hazards. John shares his extensive experience and expertise in operating heavy machinery, while Sarah brings fresh perspectives and enthusiasm for learning.

Together, they embark on collaborative projects, such as conducting safety audits and implementing preventive measures. Through regular check-in meetings, they reflect on their progress, address challenges, and celebrate successes. As a result of their partnership, both John and Sarah developed a deeper understanding of workplace safety principles and foster a culture of teamwork and communication within their department.

Their collaboration sets a positive example for the entire organization, encouraging other departments to explore similar initiatives to leverage the knowledge and talent of employees across different generations. Overall, the mentorship program proves to be instrumental in promoting a culture of continuous learning and improvement while enhancing workplace safety at the company.

This scenario offers a glimpse into the potential effectiveness of such a system when implemented in the right environment. Recent research supports this notion, with a survey conducted by AARP revealing that "83 percent of business leaders believe multigenerational workforces are essential for the growth and long-term success of their companies." Additionally, an analysis published in the journal of the American Psychological

Association indicates that managers surveyed by the Society for Human Resource Management noted that age diversity has a positive impact on organizational performance (The Power of Multigenerational Teams in the Social Sector (SSIR), n.d.).

These findings underscore the significance of intergenerational teams, emphasizing that they are not only integral to the overall health and safety of the workplace but also crucial for determining which companies will remain open and competitive in the future.

CHAPTER 4: DIFFERENCES IN SAFETY TRAINING

"Culture is what we learn from our people, and it's specific to the group you belong to, and – as I said, it's all learned," - **Elaine Cullen Vandervert**

After years of working with various teams, I've conducted safety training in all forms: from in-person, hands-on sessions in facilities teaching workers how to operate equipment safely, to online safety training during the COVID-19 pandemic, even in virtual settings. Through this extensive experience, I've noticed distinct generational differences in how different age groups perceive safety training in the workplace, particularly in its delivery.

In my role, I've had the opportunity to train over 2,000 different teams and work closely with each generational cohort, including Traditionalists, Baby Boomers, Generation Xers, Millennials, and Generation Zers. This hands-on experience has provided valuable insights into how each group approaches safety training and the various preferences they have when it comes to learning and engagement. When conducting safety education training, I've noticed distinct preferences among different generational groups. Traditionalists and Baby Boomers often prefer completing safety education onsite, in a face-to-face environment. They thrive in small group settings, where they can share experiences and stories, and are more likely to connect verbally.

These individuals typically have a strong understanding of their companies and offer valuable insights into how the workplace has evolved over time. They also appreciate tangible training materials, such as paper handouts, business cards, or brochures, which they can take back to the workplace for reference.

However, Traditionalists and Baby Boomers may struggle with virtual or remote training due to challenges with internet connectivity, difficulties logging in, or navigating online platforms' features like screen sharing, emojis, private chat, or mute buttons.

In contrast, Generation Xers demonstrate a more adaptable approach to safety training. They tend to fare well in both onsite and virtual training environments. With a solid understanding of their workplace dynamics and business operations,

Generation Xers navigate training sessions with ease, leveraging their familiarity with technology while also valuing face-to-face interactions when necessary.

Millennials and Generation Zers exhibit distinct preferences and behaviors in safety training compared to other generations. These groups excel in online or virtual training environments, embracing features like emojis and private chat to actively participate. They appreciate the flexibility and convenience offered by online training platforms, where they can comfortably share their thoughts, feelings, and actions through digital communication channels.

Providing websites and online support materials resonates well with Millennials and Generation Zers, who thrive in both small and large online group settings. They value the option to turn off their cameras for privacy while still engaging in discussions.

However, these groups may face challenges in traditional face-to-face training settings, particularly in large group settings. They often struggle with paper handouts, business cards, or brochures, which are prone to being discarded or forgotten after training sessions. Instructors should consider alternative approaches, such as providing barcodes or online resources that can be easily accessed and shared digitally, catering to Millennials' and Generation Zers' preference for digital interactions and information consumption.

To address generational differences in safety training, leaders must adopt a multifaceted approach that caters to the diverse preferences of each generation. First and foremost, offering safety training in multiple formats, including both online and on-site in-person sessions, is essential to accommodate the needs and preferences of all generations.

Additionally, employers should proactively survey their teams to gain insights into which training delivery methods work best for different generations. Based on this feedback, leaders can develop a tailored training strategy that incorporates a mix of online and in-person sessions to effectively reach all team members.

Moreover, it's crucial to implement a development plan aimed at equipping each generation with the necessary skills to utilize various workplace training technologies effectively. This may involve providing comprehensive training on how to navigate and leverage the features of selected training platforms, ensuring that all employees feel confident and proficient in using the technology.

Furthermore, instructors conducting face-to-face training sessions should consider implementing strategies to enhance engagement, particularly for Millennials and Generation Zers. This could include incorporating interactive activities, utilizing multimedia resources, and creating opportunities for open discussions to make the training sessions more dynamic and participatory for younger generations.

By adopting these measures, leaders can bridge the gap between generational differences and create a cohesive and inclusive safety training environment that resonates with all team members, ultimately fostering a culture of safety and compliance across the organization.

Here are some tips for companies to make safety training more engaging in a multi-generational workplace:

Utilize Multimedia Resources:

Incorporating multimedia elements such as videos, animations, and interactive presentations can cater to different learning preferences across generations. Visual learners may benefit from dynamic graphics and videos, while interactive elements like quizzes and simulations can engage kinesthetic learners. By diversifying the training content, companies can appeal to a broader range of learning styles and enhance overall engagement.

Gamify the Training Process:

Gamification adds an element of fun and competition to safety training, motivating employees to actively participate and learn. Employers can introduce gamified elements such as leaderboards, badges, and rewards for completing training modules or demonstrating safety knowledge. Gamified activities provide immediate feedback and encourage continuous improvement, making the learning process more engaging and enjoyable for all generations.

Encourage Active Participation:

Creating opportunities for active participation during safety training sessions can foster engagement and collaboration among employees of different generations. Group discussions, case studies, and role-playing exercises allow participants to share insights, ask questions, and apply safety concepts in real-world scenarios. Encouraging active participation empowers employees to take ownership of their learning and facilitates knowledge sharing across generations.

Provide Hands-On Demonstrations:

Hands-on demonstrations and practical exercises offer a tangible learning experience that resonates with employees across generations. By allowing participants to practice safety procedures, use equipment, and respond to simulated scenarios, companies reinforce learning objectives and build essential skills. Hands-on activities promote experiential learning, which is particularly effective for kinesthetic learners who prefer learning by doing.

Tailor Content to Different Generations:

Recognizing the diverse preferences and communication styles of different generations is key to delivering effective safety training. Employers can tailor the content, language, and examples used in training materials to resonate with each generation's experiences and perspectives. Providing relevant and relatable content ensures that all employees feel included and engaged throughout the training process.

Offer Flexibility in Training Formats:

Offering flexibility in the format and delivery of safety training accommodates the varying schedules and preferences of employees across generations.

Providing options for online, in-person, and self-paced training allows employees to choose the format that best suits their needs and learning preferences. Flexibility in training formats empowers employees to take control of their learning experience and ensures accessibility for all generations.

Promote Intergenerational Collaboration:

Facilitating collaboration and knowledge sharing among employees of different generations fosters a culture of mutual learning and support. Pairing employees from different generations as training partners or mentors encourages cross-generational dialogue and promotes the exchange of ideas and experiences. Intergenerational collaboration enriches the learning experience and strengthens relationships within the workforce.

Seek Feedback and Adaptation:

Continuously seeking feedback from employees of all generations allows companies to refine and adapt their safety training programs to better meet the needs of the multi-generational workforce. Gathering input on training content, delivery methods, and overall effectiveness enables employers to make data-driven decisions and implement improvements over time.

By listening to employee feedback and being responsive to their evolving needs, companies can ensure that safety training remains engaging, relevant, and impactful for employees of all ages.

Companies should initiate training initiatives by acknowledging and valuing the diverse learning preferences and technological aptitudes present among different age groups. Employ a versatile blend of training methodologies, ranging from traditional in-person sessions to e-learning modules and hands-on exercises, catering to the varied learning styles across your workforce.

Infuse real-life scenarios that resonate with individuals of all generations, amplifying engagement and comprehension levels.

Ensure that the training content is meticulously crafted to be clear, concise, and easily accessible to all participants. Foster a culture of open communication, encouraging employees to exchange their experiences and insights freely, thereby promoting collaborative learning.

In scenarios where training sessions are conducted repeatedly (e.g., annually, or quarterly), consider infusing elements of surprise, novelty, and delight to introduce fresh perspectives and maintain interest levels. Incorporating new discoveries each time enhances attention and stimulates discussions around the material, averting monotony. Embrace variety, which can often be seamlessly integrated during initial production stages, at minimal costs, facilitating long-term engagement.

Exercise caution when selecting language and terminology for safety training materials, avoiding jargon that may pose comprehension challenges for certain generations. Strive for clarity and simplicity in communication to ensure universal understanding and engagement across your multi-generational workforce.

When it comes to training multi-generational teams, an often-overlooked aspect is understanding the diverse learning styles and communication preferences present among individuals. Despite companies investing significant resources into safety training each year, the effectiveness of these efforts often falls short. Studies have revealed a disheartening reality: individuals tend to forget up to 70% of what they are taught within the first 24 hours following a learning event. By the end of the week, retention rates plummeted to a mere 25%. This rapid decline in memory retention poses significant challenges for both individuals and businesses alike.

The phenomenon of forgetting in learning environments can stem from various factors, including the training style, environment, or instructor quality. However, employers also grapple with learning challenges such as dyslexia, dysgraphia, and dyscalculia, which significantly impact individuals' ability to comprehend and retain information. Dyslexia, for instance, affects approximately 20% of the workforce, according to current workplace statistics. (Al-Lamki L. 2012).

A survey examining dyslexia's effects on UK registered nurses' career progression revealed its negative impact on working practices and career advancement, highlighting the lack of understanding surrounding this condition. Functional illiteracy, a prevalent issue in some societies like the USA, is estimated to affect 20% of the population, with half of these individuals having dyslexia.

Alarmingly, dyslexic individuals constitute 80% of all diagnosed learning disabilities cases. Moreover, dyslexia are often linked to higher juvenile offender rates, with 85% of juvenile offenders reported to have reading disabilities. Regrettably, I am among these statistics, having discovered my dyslexia in my twenties, well into my career, after completing college, starting a family, and navigating through life's challenges. This revelation shed light on why I faced daily struggles in my career due to my unique learning style. (Al-Lamki L. 2012).

Imagine being a new employee, eager to learn, but attending a safety training session where you're required to arrive early in the morning for an 8-hour session filled with dry, crowded PowerPoint slides delivered by an instructor who's struggling to maintain his voice. As the hours drag on, you find yourself watching the clock, your mind drifting, just wishing for the training to end. You're willing to say or do anything just to get through it, and by the end of the day, most of what you heard has been forgotten.

This scenario highlights the kind of sensory overload I've witnessed. Now, consider being in this situation with a learning disability like dyslexia, further hindering your ability to absorb information and engage effectively. That was me.

To foster a more inclusive environment for individuals facing learning challenges such as dyslexia, companies can implement the following strategies:

Provide Written Material in Different Formats:

Offer training materials in various formats, such as audio recordings, videos, and interactive online modules, in addition to traditional written documents. This caters to different learning styles and helps dyslexic individuals access information more easily.

Use Plain Language and Visual Aids: Simplify language and use clear, concise instructions in training materials. Incorporate visual aids like diagrams, charts, and infographics to reinforce key concepts and make information easier to understand.

Allow Extra Time for Training:

Recognize that dyslexic individuals may need additional time to process information and complete training activities. Offer flexible scheduling options or extended time allowances for completing safety training requirements.

Offer Dyslexia-Friendly Technology:

Utilize dyslexia-friendly fonts, such as Arial, Verdana, or OpenDyslexic, in written materials. Provide access to text-to-speech software or speech recognition tools to assist dyslexic workers in reading and comprehending written content.

Provide Personalized Support:

Assign a mentor or trainer to work closely with dyslexic employees during safety training sessions. Offer one-on-one assistance, clarifications, and additional explanations as needed to ensure comprehension and retention of the material.

Create a Supportive Environment:

Foster an inclusive workplace culture where dyslexic individuals feel comfortable seeking help and accommodations for their learning needs. Encourage open communication and provide opportunities for employees to voice their concerns or ask questions about safety training.

Offer Regular Review and Reinforcement:

Implement periodic reviews and assessments to reinforce key safety concepts and ensure ongoing learning. Provide opportunities for dyslexic workers to practice and apply their knowledge in real-world scenarios to enhance retention and proficiency.

By implementing these strategies, companies can create safety training programs that are more inclusive and accessible for dyslexic workers, ultimately promoting a safer and more supportive work environment for all employees.

In closing, embracing diversity and inclusivity isn't just about meeting regulatory requirements; it's about fostering a culture of respect, understanding, and support. By acknowledging and accommodating the unique needs of individuals, such as those with differences, we not only enhance safety training effectiveness but also cultivate a workplace where every member feels valued and empowered.

As we continue to strive for excellence in safety and compliance, let us remember that our greatest strength lies in our ability to embrace and celebrate our differences, turning them into opportunities for growth and success.

CHAPTER 5: COLLBRATION AMONG LEADERS

"A genuine leader is not a searcher for consensus but a molder of consensus." - **MLK**

In today's dynamic landscape, leaders are continually adapting to the evolving demands of the world. While much attention is often placed on the multigenerational dynamics among those being managed or on the frontline, it's essential to recognize that similar shifts are occurring within management and leadership roles.

By 2025, an estimated 75 percent of the global workforce will be comprised of Millennials, a demographic trend expected to escalate as Baby Boomers transition into retirement. In the United States alone, the turnover rate among Millennials amounts to a staggering $30.5 billion annually. Additionally, with 43 percent of Millennials contemplating early retirement, it's evident that managers who prioritize understanding and supporting their development will reap significant benefits (Magazine, 2023).

As the largest generation in today's workforce, Millennials bring with them distinct expectations and values that diverge from traditional office cultures. They challenge conventional leadership paradigms and prioritize aspects such as communication, relationship-building, and empowerment in their professional lives.

Successfully leading an organization staffed with Millennials requires a deep understanding of their desires, needs, and expectations. By embracing these insights, leaders can foster a workplace environment that resonates with this generation, driving enhanced engagement, productivity, and overall success.

Millennial leaders bring a distinct set of values and traits to the table, reshaping traditional leadership models. One of their core values is the emphasis on relationship-building and teamwork. Unlike individualistic approaches favored by previous generations, millennial leaders prioritize collaboration and seek input from their teams before making significant decisions (Post, 2024).

Moreover, millennial leaders are characterized by their willingness to speak out and challenge the status quo. Unlike their predecessors who may have adhered strictly to organizational norms, millennial leaders are more vocal about areas of dissatisfaction and are open to implementing new methods and processes. They leverage innovative communication tools such as text messaging and social media to engage with their teams and promote their organization's products (Post, 2024).

Furthermore, millennial leaders exhibit a strong commitment to diversity, purpose, and fulfillment. Having grown up in a more inclusive society, they are more inclined to prioritize diversity in their hiring practices and seek candidates from various backgrounds. Additionally, they believe in the importance of aligning with a higher purpose and expect their employers to share their values. For millennials, it's not just about avoiding harm; they strive to make a positive impact on the world and expect their organizations to do the same (Post, 2024).

Baby Boomers

Baby Boomers Baby boomers are those born between 1946 and 1964 and have been in the workforce for decades. While many are still working today, research from Gallup in 2015 found that many are starting to retire. About 50 percent of boomers aged 60 are still working, and only about one-third of those between the ages of 67 and 68 are still in the workforce.

What employees think Baby boomers tend to be seen as the keepers of traditional workplace values: loyalty, progression up the career ladder over time, hierarchy, and the expectation the company will reward them for their contribution. While these leaders have the most experience, their younger peers think they are stuck in the past when it comes to technology and leadership style.

In fact, a survey of professionals ages 45 to 74 conducted by AARP in 2013 found 64 percent of these individuals said they have experienced ageism at work or when looking for a new job.

At the same time, baby boomers can be biased against leaders from younger generations who favor building relationships with employees and informal workplace policies.

What They're Really Like

In reality, most baby boomers do believe in a traditional workplace hierarchy, favor formal policies, and take a more hands-off approach to leadership. And while they may be slower to implement new technology, most recognize the value it can bring to managing the workforce and the business as a whole.

Leadership Strengths

Baby boomers have spent the most time in the workplace overall, meaning they have the most experience in their industry and in management. Many have been with their organization for decades, giving them a strong understanding of its inner workings. They know the business and culture, allowing them to make informed decisions that will benefit their teams and the bottom line.

In addition, these professionals have benefited from the most leadership development opportunities. They've had the time and resources to grow and improve their leadership skills.

Leadership Weaknesses

While baby boomers are the most experienced group of leaders, they can be slow to recognize the need for change in the workplace.

When Vital Smarts surveyed 1,200 employees in July 2016, they found that while leaders want to believe they've created environments filled with innovation and teamwork, employees think the workplace is one of obedience, competition, and predictability.

In addition, senior executives surveyed by SuccessFactors were much more likely to be confident in their company's ability to recruit skilled workers, develop talent for the digital workplace, and plan for succession than millennial executives. And it's no surprise that only 37 percent of millennials in the same survey said senior management is proficient in using technology for competitive advantage.

Because baby boomers favor a traditional workplace hierarchy, leaders are chosen and promoted based on tenure with the company -- instead of skills, performance, and leadership potential. In fact, 76 percent of employees surveyed by Grovo said ineffective managers at their company are frequently rewarded or promoted.

Interesting Takeaways

Baby boomers may have the most experience in leadership, but that doesn't mean they know everything. Leaders in this generation should still acknowledge the evolving landscape of the workplace and adapt accordingly. While baby boomers are known for their traditional values and hierarchical approach to leadership, they must recognize the importance of embracing change, especially in the realm of technology and evolving leadership styles.

Despite being perceived as being slow to adopt new technology and informal workplace policies, many baby boomers understand the value that technology brings to the workforce and the overall business operations. They bring a wealth of experience and knowledge, having spent decades in the workforce and often within the same organization.

Generation X

Generation X, typically born in the mid-1960s through the late 1970s and early 1980s, once dominated the workforce, comprising 84 percent of it in 2008 according to Pew Research. However, their majority was overtaken by millennials in 2015, leaving Generation X in a unique position within the workplace hierarchy.

Despite being sandwiched between the prominent baby boomer generation, often their superiors, and the burgeoning millennial cohort, who are rapidly ascending the corporate ladder, Generation X possesses significant leadership potential. In a survey conducted by Future Workplace in 2015, 51 percent of respondents affirmed that Generation X employees are the most capable generation to lead organizations, highlighting their often-overlooked strengths.

Generation X individuals typically exhibit values and leadership styles that bridge the gap between baby boomers and millennials. Having observed the workaholic tendencies of baby boomers, they prioritize work-life balance over relentless career advancement. Consequently, as leaders, they prioritize results over mere hours spent on projects and value quality work over quantity. Furthermore, Generation X leaders tend to foster a more relaxed and open work environment, favoring transparency and accessibility over rigid hierarchical structures.

However, despite their strengths, Generation X leaders still face challenges, particularly in terms of experience and development. A survey by Grovo revealed that 98 percent of middle managers feel their company's managers require more training, while 87 percent expressed a desire for more training themselves when they initially assumed leadership roles.

In conclusion, Generation X holds immense leadership potential but requires further experience and development to fully harness it. Opportunities for shadowing senior leadership and investing in learning and development initiatives can help bridge existing skill gaps and empower Generation X leaders to realize their full potential in guiding organizations through an increasingly complex business landscape.

Millennials

Although there is no official definition, millennials are typically considered those born between 1980 and 1997. Despite being perceived as newcomers to the workplace by older generations, more than a third of American workers today are millennials, as per data from Pew Research.

Perceptions of Millennials in the Workplace

Much has been said about millennials, and opinions about this generation vary. Generally, older generations view millennials as entitled professionals who rely excessively on technology. For instance, 85 percent of millennials surveyed by Gallup access the internet from their phones, a higher percentage than any other generation.

However, this reliance on technology isn't universally seen as negative. In fact, Generation X and baby boomers surveyed by Workfront rated millennials as the most tech-savvy and creative at work. Yet, they also perceived millennials as the least cooperative, least likely to take responsibility, and the biggest complainers.

Despite being a significant portion of the workforce, millennials are still viewed as inexperienced. A study published in the Journal of Organizational Behavior in April 2016 found that younger managers face a heightened risk of rejection due to perceived lack of expertise and status. Nevertheless, millennials possess unique strengths and weaknesses in leadership.

Characteristics of Millennials

Millennials are ambitious and eager to assume leadership roles to drive significant changes in the workplace. They have faith in technology's transformative potential, prioritize innovation, and emphasize mentoring and leadership development.

While still considered newcomers in many workplaces, numerous millennials are already assuming leadership roles, effecting changes, and leading older generations. In fact, a survey by executive development firm Future Workplace and career networking company Beyond.com found that 83 percent of respondents observed millennials managing individuals from Generation X and baby boomer cohorts.

Strengths of Millennial Leaders

Millennial leaders are more attuned to employee needs compared to older generations. According to a survey by Deloitte, millennials worldwide believe that employee satisfaction, loyalty, and fair treatment are essential for long-term business success. They adopt an inclusive and empathetic leadership style, drawing from their recent experiences as team members.

This employee-centric approach drives millennial leaders to advocate for changing traditional practices across their organizations. For instance, a survey by SuccessFactors revealed that 38 percent of millennial leaders allocate resources to train the next generation of leaders, compared to 48 percent of senior leaders. They recognize the importance of development opportunities at all organizational levels, promoting fairness and benefiting the organization with better leaders.

Moreover, while older generations may be more entrenched in traditional practices, millennial leaders are more likely to challenge them. The same SuccessFactors survey indicated that millennial executives express less confidence in their organization's ability to develop talent for the digital workplace and plan for succession compared to their older counterparts.

Weaknesses of Millennial Leaders

Despite their drive for organizational change, many millennial leaders feel inadequately equipped with the necessary skills. The Deloitte survey found that 63 percent of millennials believe their leadership skills are not fully developed. Additionally, leading older employees can be challenging for over one-third of millennials surveyed by Future Workplace and Beyond.com, highlighting the persistence of traditional workplace hierarchies.

Moreover, millennials aren't alone in feeling unprepared for leadership positions; older generations share similar sentiments. In the same survey by Future Workplace and Beyond.com, 45 percent of baby boomer and Gen X respondents expressed concerns about millennials' lack of managerial experience negatively impacting company culture.

Key Takeaways

Despite facing criticism, millennials exhibit innovative leadership qualities and challenge traditional workplace norms. However, they still need to refine their leadership skills. Expanding learning and development opportunities and seeking guidance from older leaders, even if their methods seem outdated, can facilitate the transformation of inventive millennials into effective and dynamic leaders.

Generation Z

Generation Z, typically defined as those born in the late 1990s through the early 2010s, represents the younger cohort gradually entering the workforce. While most are still in school, this generation holds the future of the workplace.

Perceptions of Generation Z in the Workplace

Despite being newcomers to the workforce, older generations have already formed opinions about Generation Z. Raised in the digital era with internet, social media, and smartphones, older professionals often anticipate poor communication skills from this generation. Additionally, due to their youth, Generation Z is viewed as inexperienced and naive, with attributes like laziness and entitlement being associated with them as more enter the workplace.

Characteristics of Generation Z Employees

In terms of their preferences and needs, Generation Z employees share similarities with millennials. Both cohorts, according to a report from Randstad, show similar preferences regarding work environment and communication styles. Moreover, both generations prioritize communication as the most important quality in a leader. Despite lacking the extensive experience of older generations, Generation Z is characterized by ambition and a strong desire for learning and development opportunities, alongside an excitement for new technology and its impact on workplace efficiency.

Strengths in Leadership

Contrary to the perception of struggling with communication, Generation Z exhibits strengths in face-to-face communication, as revealed by studies. They also prefer more inclusive leadership styles and value qualities such as supportiveness, honesty, confidence, and approachability in leaders. Although they have yet to reach leadership positions in significant numbers, Generation Z displays eagerness for such opportunities, with a notable desire to start businesses and hire others.

Challenges in Leadership Growth

While inclusive leadership styles, often perceived as strengths among older leaders, can sometimes be viewed as weaknesses by younger leaders, particularly those from Generation Z. Research suggests that when young managers actively seek input from their teams, it may inadvertently signal inexperience to their employees, potentially diminishing their perceived effectiveness as leaders.

Compounding this issue is the stark reality revealed by LinkedIn's research: one in five Gen Z workers reported not having engaged in a single direct conversation with someone over the age of 50 in their workplace over the past year. Furthermore, they expressed the lowest confidence levels in interacting with individuals from other generations.

In contrast, only 17% of the 1000 British workers surveyed by LinkedIn admitted to feeling unsure about approaching colleagues of different age groups. While the exact reasons behind Gen Z's struggle to connect with their senior peers remain unclear, previous analyses have suggested that the lack of shared life experiences, such as marriage, parenthood, or pet ownership, may contribute to this disconnect.

Regardless of the root cause, the absence of meaningful interactions with older colleagues could have detrimental effects on the career advancement prospects of Gen Z workers. Research consistently highlights the importance of face time with management in building rapport and increasing the likelihood of receiving promotions or salary raises.

Interestingly, while Gen Z workers acknowledge the potential benefits of cultivating relationships with their senior counterparts, many are hesitant to take proactive steps in this regard. LinkedIn's findings indicate that 64% of Gen Z employees are waiting for their companies to initiate efforts to foster intergenerational collaboration, despite recognizing the value of such interactions in enhancing productivity and learning.

However, it's not just Gen Z who prefer interacting within their own age group. Approximately 40% of workers over the age of 55 reported not having spoken to a Gen Z colleague in the past year, indicating a mutual reluctance to bridge the generational divide. This reluctance may stem from a variety of factors, including differing communication styles, perceptions, and interests.

Ultimately, while engaging in casual conversation may seem like a simple task, it's evident that it is one of many "basic" soft skills that Gen Z may have missed out on developing, particularly amidst the isolation imposed by the pandemic. Recognizing these challenges and actively working to overcome them is essential for fostering a more inclusive and collaborative work environment for employees of all generations. (1 In 5 Gen Zers Haven't Had a

Single Conversation with Someone Over 50 in Their Workplace in the Last Year, LinkedIn Research Says, 2024)

Key Takeaways

Despite their relative lack of experience, Generation Z demonstrates an understanding of effective leadership in today's workplace. With increased confidence and a more directive leadership approach, they will be poised to assume leadership roles as opportunities arise. Each generation possesses its own unique strengths and areas for growth in leadership.

By recognizing these differences and being open to learning from one another, leaders across generations can enhance their effectiveness and create more balanced leadership teams. Rather than hastily judging other generations, leaders should embrace diversity and collaborate on developing their individual skills.

Here are some key points to consider as you think about working with others that are part of your generation and other generations:

Interacting with Co-workers of Your Generation:

1. *Recognize Diversity:* Understand that even within your generation, there will be diversity in backgrounds, experiences, and perspectives. Avoid making assumptions based solely on age.
2. *Adaptability:* Be open to different work styles and approaches within your generation. Not everyone will share the same preferences or methods for completing tasks.
3. *Communication:* Foster open and transparent communication channels among peers. Utilize digital platforms and social media, which may be more familiar to your generation, but also be open to in-person or phone conversations when necessary.

Interacting with Co-workers of Other Generations:

1. *Respect Differences:* Acknowledge and appreciate the diverse perspectives and experiences that colleagues from other generations bring to the table. Avoid stereotypes or assumptions about their abilities or preferences.

2. *Learn from Experience:* Be receptive to learning from older colleagues who may have valuable experience and wisdom to share. Seek mentorship opportunities to gain insights into different approaches to work and problem-solving.
3. *Flexibility*: Be adaptable in your communication and collaboration styles when working with colleagues from other generations. Recognize that preferences for communication methods or work processes may vary.

Steps for Better Understanding and Collaboration:

1. *Engage in Active Listening*: Take the time to listen and understand the perspectives and concerns of colleagues from different generations. Ask questions and seek clarification to ensure clear communication.
2. *Foster a Culture of Learning*: Create opportunities for intergenerational learning and knowledge sharing within the workplace. Encourage mentorship programs, cross-generational team projects, or skill-sharing sessions.
3. *Embrace Feedback*: Solicit feedback from colleagues of all generations to gain insights

into how you can improve collaboration and communication. Be open to constructive criticism and willing to make adjustments.
4. *Lead by Example:* Demonstrate inclusive behavior and respect for all colleagues, regardless of their age. Encourage a culture of mutual respect and collaboration within your team or organization.

Expectations for Work Processes:

- *Flexibility*: Recognize that different generations may have varying expectations for how work gets done. Embrace flexibility in approaches to tasks and projects, focusing on outcomes rather than rigid processes.
- *Embrace Technology*: Leverage technology to streamline work processes and enhance collaboration, particularly for younger generations who may be more tech-savvy. Provide training and support for colleagues who may be less familiar with digital tools.

Expectations for Communication:

1. *Clear Communication Channels*: Establish clear communication channels that accommodate the preferences of colleagues from different

generations. Offer multiple avenues for communication, including email, phone, video conferencing, and in-person meetings.
2. *Respectful Communication*: Foster a culture of respectful and inclusive communication, where all voices are heard and valued. Avoid language or behaviors that may be perceived as disrespectful or dismissive.

Expectations for Communication with Leaders:

1. *Open Door Policy*: Encourage leaders to maintain an open-door policy, welcoming input and feedback from employees of all generations. Create opportunities for transparent communication and constructive dialogue between leaders and their teams.
2. Mutual Respect: Foster a culture of mutual respect between leaders and employees, regardless of age. Encourage leaders to listen attentively, consider diverse perspectives, and provide guidance and support as needed.

Expectations for Promotion:

1. *Skill-Based Evaluation*: Advocate for promotion criteria that are based on skills, performance, and merit rather than tenure or age. Encourage a fair and transparent promotion process that rewards competence and contributions.
2. *Professional Development*: Support opportunities for professional development and career advancement for employees of all generations. Emphasize the importance of ongoing learning and skill-building to prepare employees for future opportunities.

When contemplating the collaboration of multigenerational leaders within the workplace, I'm reminded of the sitcom "The Neighborhood," where Cedric the Entertainer portrays Calvin Butler, a seasoned 65-year-old retired auto machinist turned business partner alongside his son, Marcel Spears, who embodies Marty Butler, a tech-savvy young entrepreneur managing their electric vehicle repair shop.

In the show, Calvin assumes the role of a strict, authoritative boss, while Marty adopts a more empathetic approach, investing time in understanding and connecting with his team, even providing amenities like a foosball table. However, Calvin's insistence on separating personal activities like foosball from work tasks leads to conflict, prompting questions about the dynamics of leadership.

Their relationship is emblematic of the clash between traditional leadership values and modern workplace expectations. Calvin, having grown up in a different era, values discipline, and productivity above all else, viewing the workplace as a space solely for work-related activities. In contrast, Marty recognizes the importance of fostering a positive work culture, where employees feel valued and supported beyond their professional duties.

As Marty's efforts to foster genuine connections are undermined by his father's detachment, employees become disheartened. The foosball table, once intended to foster camaraderie and relaxation during breaks, becomes a point of contention. Calvin's insistence on strictly delineating work and leisure time leads to frustration and disillusionment among the employees.

Feeling disconnected and undervalued, some employees begin to seek opportunities elsewhere, drawn to companies where they feel appreciated and where their personal well-being is prioritized. This turnover not only impacts team morale but also affects the shop's competitiveness, as talented individuals depart for rival businesses.

This scenario prompts reflection on the importance of leaders understanding the intrinsic value of workplace connections and the impact it has on team morale and productivity. It highlights the need for leaders to adapt to changing workplace dynamics and embrace a more inclusive and empathetic leadership style to foster a thriving work environment.

Regrettably, many workplaces grapple with these challenges, particularly among leaders themselves. When discussing these issues, it's crucial to reflect on how connected our leaders truly are and whether they are learning from one another to foster a safe and healthy workplace environment. Are they engaging in activities outside of work, such as attending barbecues or playing softball in the park, to build personal relationships?

Do they take the time to learn about each other's families and what matters most to them beyond their professional roles? Are they forging genuine connections on a human level, rather than solely viewing each other as colleagues?

In parallel with creating a supportive workplace culture, it is imperative for leaders to engage in collaborative mentoring among themselves. This entails sharing experiences and knowledge regarding interpersonal dynamics, handling difficult situations, and implementing creative solutions to motivate and maintain a cohesive team in the face of evolving workplace challenges. By fostering a culture of mutual support and learning among leaders, organizations can strengthen their leadership effectiveness and enhance overall workplace well-being.

CHAPTER 6: CULTURE AMONG GENERATIONS

"Try not to become a person of success but rather try to become a person of value." – **Albert Einstein**

Throughout my leadership journey, I've traversed various workplaces, spanning industries both big and small. One observation remains consistent: many organizations strive to enhance workplace functionality, safety, and productivity through the adoption of principles and strategies. There's a tendency to seek answers from other companies, hoping to emulate their success. However, it's crucial to recognize that culture cannot be purchased off the shelf.

While companies may attempt to buy into the culture of others, it's essential to understand that true culture cannot be bought—it must be painstakingly crafted. Culture is not a commodity that can be repackaged and sold; rather, it is the essence of an organization, woven into its fabric by its people and their collective values and behaviors. It's the foundation upon which performance is built, influencing how teams interact and ultimately dictating their success.

In essence, attempting to buy culture is akin to expecting to purchase a fully furnished house and expecting it to feel like home without investing the time and effort to personalize it. Just as a house becomes a home through the memories and experiences shared within its walls, a company's culture is shaped by the daily interactions and shared values of its employees.

In today's multi-generational landscape, envisioning a robust and flourishing safety culture is imperative. As an avid reader of business magazines, I often delve into the narratives of companies celebrated for earning accolades such as "Best Place to Work" or recognition for fostering the "Safest Workplace." These distinguished organizations are lauded for their ability to cultivate environments where employees not only feel content and secure but also consistently show up with enthusiasm and dedication.

What sets these companies apart? What distinguishes them from the rest? In my view, the defining factor lies in their organizational culture, the way people talk and treat each other. It's the cornerstone upon which their success is built.

For these exemplary companies, a strong safety culture isn't merely a set of policies or procedures; it's a shared mindset woven into the fabric of daily operations. It's a commitment to prioritizing the well-being of every individual, regardless of age or background. It's about fostering an environment where safety is everyone's responsibility, and open dialogue is encouraged.

In these organizations, communication flows freely, and employees feel empowered to voice concerns, share insights, and collaborate on solutions. There's a palpable sense of trust and mutual respect, where individuals know that their well-being matters and that their contributions are valued.

Ultimately, what sets these companies apart is their unwavering dedication to nurturing a culture where every voice is heard, and every individual feels valued and supported. It's a culture where safety isn't just a priority—it's a way of life. And it's this commitment to fostering a positive and inclusive environment that truly makes them stand out in today's competitive landscape.

In a strong safety culture, communication serves as the cornerstone of the entire framework. It's not just about exchanging information; it's about fostering an environment where every voice is heard, valued, and respected. Employees feel empowered to speak up about safety concerns, knowing that their input is welcomed and taken seriously.

Conversations in this culture are characterized by transparency, meaning that information about safety protocols, incident reports, and risk assessments is readily accessible to all employees. This transparency builds trust and confidence in the organization's commitment to safety.

Moreover, communication in a strong safety culture is not one-sided. It's a two-way street where employees are encouraged to actively participate in safety initiatives and decision-making processes. This involvement creates a sense of ownership and accountability for safety outcomes, motivating individuals to take personal responsibility for their actions and the well-being of their colleagues.

In addition to being transparent and participatory, communication in a strong safety culture is also constructive and solution oriented. Instead of dwelling on problems or assigning blame, discussions focus on identifying root causes and implementing effective solutions. Feedback is welcomed as a valuable tool for continuous improvement, and employees are encouraged to learn from mistakes and share best practices with their peers.

Overall, communication in a strong safety culture fosters a sense of community, where employees feel supported, respected, and empowered to contribute to the organization's safety goals. It's a culture where safety is not just a priority, but a shared value that permeates every aspect of the workplace.

Conversely, in a poor safety culture, communication is often characterized by silence, avoidance, or indifference towards safety issues. Employees may feel discouraged from speaking up about safety concerns due to a perceived lack of support or a fear of reprisal. This lack of communication creates a culture of secrecy and mistrust, where safety issues are swept under the rug rather than addressed openly and transparently.

Moreover, in a poor safety culture, communication tends to be one-sided and top-down, with little opportunity for employee input or feedback. Decisions about safety policies and procedures are made without consulting those who are directly affected by them, leading to frustration and disengagement among employees.

Conversations about safety in a poor safety culture are often met with resistance or defensiveness, as management may be unwilling to acknowledge or address systemic issues. This defensive posture further undermines trust and confidence in the organization's commitment to safety, creating a vicious cycle of apathy and complacency.

Overall, communication in a poor safety culture serves to perpetuate the status quo rather than drive meaningful change. It's a culture where safety is seen as a nuisance rather than a priority, and employees feel powerless to effect positive change.

One thought-provoking question that often arises is: How can organizational leaders bridge generational gaps to cultivate a safety culture that resonates with employees of all ages? Indeed, the concept of safety has evolved significantly over the past decades. Consider the signing of the Occupational Safety and Health Act by President Nixon over 50 years ago on December 29, 1970. At that time, life-saving technologies, detailed inspection systems, electronic job hazard analyses, drone surveillance, and wearable technology for tracking workers' vital signs or emotions were not commonplace. The workplace primarily relied on paper-based systems, and safety measures were often reactive rather than proactive.

Even today, some companies continue to grapple with challenges related to worker exhaustion and hazardous working conditions that pose significant risks to employees. This underscores the importance of establishing a robust safety culture tailored to the modern workforce.

However, the question remains: How can this be accomplished? The truth is, building a strong safety culture is neither a quick fix nor an overnight endeavor. It requires a considerable investment of time, resources, and unwavering commitment from organizational leaders. Furthermore, selecting the right individuals to lead and champion safety initiatives is paramount to success.

To address the question of how organizational leaders can bridge generational gaps to create a culture of safety that resonates with employees across all age groups, consider the following strategies:

Understand Generational Differences:

Understanding the diverse perspectives and priorities of different generations is crucial for developing effective safety initiatives. Organizational leaders can conduct research, surveys, or focus groups to gain insights into the safety attitudes and perceptions of employees across various age groups.

Workshops or training sessions can be organized to educate leaders and employees about generational differences and their impact on safety practices. By tailoring safety communication materials, such as training modules or safety policies, to resonate with the values and priorities of each generation, organizations can create a more inclusive and effective safety culture.

Promote Communication and Collaboration:

Fostering open and transparent communication is essential for creating a culture of safety that resonates with employees of all ages. Consider a manufacturing plant where employees work in different shifts and departments. In this scenario, there is limited interaction between workers from various age groups, leading to silos and communication barriers. As a result, safety concerns may go unaddressed, and valuable insights from experienced workers may not be shared with younger employees. Without a platform for open dialogue and collaboration, employees may feel isolated and reluctant to voice their safety concerns or ideas for improvement. This lack of communication can hinder the organization's ability to identify and mitigate safety risks effectively, ultimately compromising workplace safety and employee well-being.

By promoting communication and collaboration across all levels and departments, organizations can break down silos, foster teamwork, and create a supportive environment where safety is everyone's responsibility.

Organizations should establish easy to use platforms or forums where employees feel comfortable sharing safety concerns, ideas, and best practices without fear of judgment. Cross-functional teams comprising members from different generations can collaborate on safety initiatives and projects, bringing diverse perspectives and experiences to the table.

Regular safety meetings or huddles can provide opportunities for employees to discuss safety issues, share updates, and brainstorm solutions collaboratively, fostering a sense of teamwork and collective responsibility for safety.

Provide Comprehensive Training:

Offering comprehensive safety training programs is essential for equipping employees with the knowledge and skills they need to navigate safety hazards effectively. Organizations can provide a variety of training formats, including in-person workshops, online courses, hands-on simulations, and job shadowing experiences, to accommodate diverse learning preferences.

Incorporating real-life scenarios, case studies, and interactive activities into safety training programs can enhance engagement and retention. Assigning mentors or coaches to provide personalized guidance and support can further enhance the effectiveness of safety training and ensure that employees feel confident in their ability to follow safety protocols.

Embrace Technology:

Leveraging technology can significantly enhance safety practices and procedures in the workplace. Organizations can invest in state-of-the-art safety technologies, such as wearable devices, sensors, and predictive analytics tools, to identify potential hazards and mitigate risks in real-time.

For example, a manufacturing company may invest in wearable devices equipped with biometric sensors that monitor employees' vital signs in real-time. If a worker's heart rate or body temperature exceeds safe levels, an alert is sent to supervisors, enabling them to intervene promptly and prevent potential health issues or accidents.

Additionally, the company might deploy drones equipped with high-resolution cameras for aerial inspections of hazardous areas, allowing for remote monitoring and assessment of safety risks without exposing workers to potential dangers. By leveraging innovative technologies like these, organizations can proactively identify and address safety hazards, improve situational awareness, and enhance overall safety outcomes in the workplace.

It is critical that companies provide proper training and support to ensure that employees are proficient in using safety technology effectively and understand its role in enhancing workplace safety is essential. Additionally, fostering a culture of innovation by encouraging employees to suggest and implement new technologies or digital solutions that improve safety outcomes can drive continuous improvement in safety practices.

Lead by Example:

Leading by example is crucial for establishing a culture of safety that resonates with employees across all age groups. Organizational leaders should demonstrate a visible commitment to safety by adhering to safety protocols, wearing personal protective equipment (PPE), and actively participating in safety initiatives. Encouraging leaders to engage in safety walkthroughs, audits, and inspections to assess safety hazards firsthand and address them proactively can further reinforce the organization's commitment to safety.

When leaders demonstrate a visible commitment to safety by adhering to safety protocols and wearing personal protective equipment (PPE), they set a positive example for their teams to follow.

However, failing to comply with safety measures can undermine the organization's safety culture and erode employee trust and confidence. For example, if a leader neglects to wear safety glasses while on the factory floor, it sends a message to employees that safety is not a priority. This lack of leadership can lead to complacency among workers and increase the risk of accidents or injuries.

Also, companies should set clear and consistent communication of safety goals and expectations, emphasizing safety as a core value, is essential for ensuring alignment and accountability throughout the organization.

Encourage Intergenerational Mentorship:

Promoting intergenerational mentorship especially among management teams can facilitate knowledge transfer and skill development, fostering a culture of learning and collaboration. Organizations can establish formal mentorship programs that pair older, more experienced employees with younger, less experienced counterparts to facilitate knowledge exchange and skill development.

Encouraging reverse mentoring, where younger employees share their experiences and modern safety practices with older colleagues, can further enhance cross-generational learning. Providing resources and training to mentors and mentees to ensure the success of the mentorship relationship and maximize its impact on safety culture is essential.

Recognize and Reward Safety Excellence:

Companies should use a reward system. Recognizing and rewarding safety excellence is essential for reinforcing positive safety behaviors and fostering a culture of continuous improvement. Implementing a safety recognition program that acknowledges individuals and teams for their contributions to maintaining a safe work environment can help instill a sense of pride and ownership among employees.

Celebrating safety milestones, such as achieving certain number hazards corrected or completing safety training, with rewards, certificates, or public recognition can further motivate employees to prioritize safety in their daily activities. By recognizing and rewarding safety excellence, organizations can reinforce the importance of safety as a core value and inspire employees to uphold high safety standards.

Companies should solicit feedback from employees to ensure that recognition programs align with their preferences and motivations and adjusting them accordingly can help maintain engagement and participation over time.

To ensure that recognition programs align with employees' preferences and motivations and maintain engagement and participation over time, companies can employ several strategies to solicit feedback effectively:

- *Anonymous Surveys*: Anonymous surveys provide insights into employee preferences for recognition without fear of reprisal or bias.
- *Focus Groups*: Focus groups gather diverse employee perspectives, fostering discussions that uncover common themes and preferences regarding recognition programs.
- *One-on-One Interviews*: Individual interviews offer personalized insights into each employee's unique preferences and motivations for recognition.
- *Employee Forums or Town Halls*: Forums and town halls create inclusive environments where employees can openly

share feedback and suggestions for improving recognition efforts.

By implementing and expanding upon these strategies, organizational leaders can successfully bridge generational divides and cultivate a safety culture that not only prioritizes the well-being of employees but also encourages collaboration, innovation, and ongoing enhancement across all age groups in the workplace.

By recognizing the diverse perspectives and preferences of employees from different generations, leaders can tailor safety initiatives to resonate with each demographic, ensuring that safety practices are understood and embraced by all.

Furthermore, fostering open communication channels and providing opportunities for intergenerational mentorship can facilitate knowledge sharing and skill development, fostering a sense of camaraderie and shared responsibility for safety among employees of all ages.

Through continuous improvement efforts and a commitment to leveraging technological advancements, organizations can stay ahead of evolving safety risks and empower employees to actively contribute to creating a safer and healthier work environment for everyone.

CHAPTER 7: THE FUTURE OF THE WORKPLACE

"We must learn to live together as brothers or perish together as fools. – Martin Luther King, Jr."

Safety in the workplace is undergoing a significant shift as organizations grapple with the complexities inherent in managing a diverse workforce spanning four different generations. This evolution is characterized by the need to navigate through stereotypes, biases, and varied backgrounds, as the modern workplace has transformed into a melting pot of individuals striving to enact change, seize opportunities, and build brighter futures for themselves and their families. The essence of true connection among employees not only fosters innovation but also cultivates an environment conducive to success and growth.

This unprecedented diversity brings forth a rich tapestry of skills, perspectives, and life experiences that can significantly enrich an organization's innovation, productivity, and overall performance. However, to harness the full potential of this multigenerational workforce and foster age-inclusive cultures, organizations must go beyond mere recognition of diversity and actively implement strategies that promote collaboration, understanding, and mutual respect among employees of all ages.

Cultivate Lifelong Learning Opportunities

In today's rapidly evolving job market, where careers can span decades, continuous learning is not just beneficial but essential to keeping job skills current and staying competitive. According to industry research only a small majority of employers (54%) place significant emphasis on professional growth and development for employees of all ages, including those 50 and older. (Collinson, 2023)

While programs such as job training (46%), mentorships (36%), and professional development initiatives (32%) are commonly cited, there is a notable lack of specific training programs addressing generational differences and age discrimination, with fewer than three in ten employers offering such programs (28%). This represents a significant missed opportunity for enhancing employee value and career progression within the organization.

By expanding on these strategies and actively investing in comprehensive training programs that address generational diversity and age-related biases, organizations can empower employees to adapt to changing workplace dynamics, foster mutual understanding, and drive collective growth and success. Through a commitment to lifelong learning and professional development, organizations can create an inclusive environment where employees of all ages feel valued, supported, and empowered to thrive.

Offer Flexible Work Arrangements

Employers often believe they provide robust support for work-life balance, yet there exists a notable disparity between this perception and the reality experienced by employees. While a staggering 96% of employers feel they are helpful in supporting their employees' quest for work-life balance, a significantly lower 75% of workers share this sentiment about their employers.

To bridge this gap and enhance employee satisfaction and retention, employers can prioritize offering flexible work arrangements. These arrangements not only promote work-life balance but also assist employees in maintaining their job performance and productivity during significant life transitions such as starting a family, caregiving responsibilities, pursuing further education, or transitioning into retirement (Collinson, 2023).

Despite the prevalence of alternative work arrangements, such as flexible work schedules and the ability to adjust work hours, relatively few employers offer a wide range of options. Forward-thinking organizations that adapt to the changing times prioritize flexible work schedules (58%), the ability to adjust work hours (51%), and hybrid work arrangements (44%). Less common offerings include unpaid leave of absence (43%), on-site work options (e.g., office, company location, WeWork) (38%), and exclusive remote work opportunities (36%). Moreover, only 35% of employers allow employees to transition between full-time and part-time roles, with just one in four offering sabbatical opportunities.

These flexible work arrangements not only benefit employees but also provide a competitive advantage for employers by expanding their talent pool. By removing geographical, transportation, scheduling, and other constraints, organizations can attract and retain top talent who may otherwise be unavailable. This expanded talent pool fosters diversity and innovation within the workforce, driving organizational success and resilience in an ever-evolving business landscape.

Support Caregiving Employees At Work

As the population ages, the number of workers assuming caregiving responsibilities for aging or ill relatives is on the rise. Currently, 36% of workers have served or are currently serving as caregivers for a relative or friend during their career, excluding parenting responsibilities. Interestingly, caregiving responsibilities are shared across generations, with Millennials being the most likely cohort (40%) to take on such roles. However, nearly nine out of ten caregiving workers have had to make adjustments to their employment, ranging from missing workdays to leaving their jobs altogether.

Employers have a significant role to play in supporting their caregiving employees, not only to preserve productivity but also to foster goodwill among all employees. The most common caregiving support programs offered by employers include unpaid leave of absence (40%), paid leave of absence (34%), online resources and tools (24%), employee assistance programs with counseling and referral services (24%), and referrals to backup care (21%). Additionally, about one in five employers provide training for both employees and managers on how to handle caregiving situations (23% and 21%, respectively) (Collinson, 2023).

With the aging population, the demand for both unpaid family caregivers and professional caregivers is expected to rise. According to a report by the Global Coalition on Aging, employers in the healthcare industry, where professional caregivers are prevalent, can play a vital role in enhancing public perceptions of the caregiving workforce. Public awareness campaigns highlighting the value of caregivers, coupled with recruitment incentives, can attract more workers to the sector.

Moreover, the industry can establish standards for training and quality, and improve working conditions by addressing worker health, work-life balance, scheduling, autonomy, pay, and career advancement opportunities. These measures can contribute to a more sustainable and supportive environment for both professional and unpaid caregivers, ultimately benefiting employees, employers, and society as a whole.

Facilitate Longer Working Lives by Offering Flexible Retirement Solutions

Today's workforce is redefining traditional notions of retirement, with many workers planning to extend their careers and transition into retirement gradually. Fifty-two percent of workers anticipate retiring at age 65 or older, or have no plans to retire at all, driven by financial considerations and a desire for healthy aging. However, despite this shifting landscape, many employers have yet to develop comprehensive options to support their employees in this transition phase.

Interestingly, offering flexible retirement options can serve as a potent tool for employee retention. Allowing for a gradual transition between work and retirement can prevent the loss of valuable employees who wish to scale back their commitments but are not yet ready for full retirement.

Unfortunately, fewer than one in three employers have established formal phased retirement programs with specific provisions and requirements for employees seeking to transition into retirement (32%). In the absence of such programs, many employers do offer alternative work-related transition options. These include flexible work schedules and arrangements (46%), opportunities for employees to reduce their hours and transition from full-time to part-time work (41%), and the option for employees to take on less demanding roles (35%), (Collinson, 2023).

Moreover, employers are missing opportunities to facilitate seamless transitions for their employees. Fewer than one in three employers actively encourage retiring employees to engage in succession planning, training, and mentoring programs (32%). Additionally, even fewer employers provide information about encore career opportunities to retiring employees (26%), (Collinson, 2023). By failing to implement these initiatives, employers risk losing valuable expertise and experience while overlooking opportunities to support their workforce's evolving needs and preferences.

Offer Comprehensive Employee Health and Retirement Benefits

Employers wield significant influence in shaping the health, well-being, and financial security of their workforce. In today's competitive labor market, a robust benefits package can serve as a critical tool for both attracting and retaining top talent.

However, employers may be undervaluing the importance workers place on employee benefits. While 95% of workers prioritize health insurance as a crucial benefit, only 63% of employers offer it. Similarly, 91% of workers value retirement savings plans like a 401(k), yet only 52% of employers provide such options, (Collinson, 2023).

Competitive benefit offerings extend beyond these basics to include life insurance, disability insurance, pension plans, workplace wellness programs, employee assistance programs, financial wellness programs, and a range of voluntary benefits.

Moreover, employers have a key role in promoting healthy aging and longevity among their workforce. Encouraging employees to prioritize their physical and mental health through preventive measures, regular screenings, and accessing care when needed can lead to a happier, healthier, and more productive workforce.

By embracing best practices and catering to the diverse needs of employees across all age groups, employers can foster a culture where employees thrive. This not only enhances business outcomes and strengthens talent recruitment and retention but also sets the stage for future success.

Employers who fail to embrace age-friendly practices risk falling behind in today's dynamic landscape. Your employees are the backbone of your organization, deserving of a safe and supportive work environment as they strive to make a living. To improve workplace safety, employers, leaders, community advocates, and policymakers must commit to continuous improvement and inclusive solutions that benefit all workers, regardless of age, gender, religion, or sexual orientation.

Remember, as a leader, you have the power to shape the future of the workplace. In the words of Martin Luther King Jr., "The ultimate measure of a man is not where he stands in moments of comfort, but where he stands at times of challenge and controversy." Proactively addressing workplace safety and inclusivity is not just a moral imperative but also a strategic decision that ensures long-term success. Embrace the opportunity to be the change you wish to see in the workplace, for the safety and well-being of all. As we conclude this journey through the intricate landscape of generational diversity in the workplace, let us reflect on the insights gained and the questions pondered.

From unraveling the impact of generational differences on attitudes towards workplace safety to exploring the most challenging issues faced by multi-generational managers, we've delved deep into the dynamics that shape our professional environments. We've examined common safety concerns across different generations and contemplated how individuals from varying age groups respond to safety training and protocols.

Through it all, one resounding theme emerges: the importance of effective communication in promoting workplace safety. Regardless of age or background, clear and comprehensive communication lies at the heart of fostering a culture of safety within organizations. It is the bridge that connects diverse perspectives and experiences, enabling collaboration, understanding, and collective action towards shared safety goals.

As we navigate the ever-evolving landscape of work, let us remember that our differences are not barriers but rather opportunities for growth and innovation. By embracing inclusivity, empathy, and open dialogue, we can create workplaces that prioritize the well-being of all employees, regardless of generation.

So, as you close this book, may you carry forward the lessons learned and the insights gained, striving to build safer, healthier, and more harmonious work environments for generations to come.

.

NOTES

1 in 5 Gen Zers haven't had a single conversation with someone over 50 in their workplace in the last year, LinkedIn research says. (2024, March 21). Fortune Europe. https://fortune.com/europe/2024/03/21/1-in-5-gen-z-workers-no-conversation-someone-over-50-workplace-last-year-linkedin-research/

AARP Research, GfK Roper, Perron, R., Rix, S., Kane-Williams, E., Egusquiza, R., Thomer, M., Nathan, D., Burns, M. L., Coates-Carter, K., Banda, D., Setzfand, J., Koenig, G., Bullock, B., Allen, E., Chalfie, D., Martin-Firvida, C., Brown, S. K., Choi-Allum, L., . . . Leslie, J. (2014). STAYING AHEAD OF THE CURVE 2013: THE AARP WORK AND CAREER STUDY. In *AARP Research*. AARP Research. http://www.aarp.org/content/dam/aarp/research/surveys_statistics/general/2014/Staying-Ahead-of-the-Curve-2013-The-Work-and-Career-Study-AARP-res-gen.pdf

Authors, C. C. (2022, July 21). *Safety culture in the workplace: How generational differences present challenges, opportunities*. Compact Equipment Magazine. https://compactequip.com/business/safety-culture-in-the-workplace-how-generational-differences-present-challenges-opportunities/

Buckley, P., Viechnicki, P., & Akrur Barua. (2016). *The 2016 Deloitte Millennial Survey*. https://www2.deloitte.com/content/dam/Deloitte/global/Documents/About-Deloitte/gx-millenial-survey-2016-exec-summary.pdf

Buengeler, C., Homan, A. C., & Voelpel, S. C. (2016a). The challenge of being a young manager: The effects of contingent reward and participative leadership on team-level turnover depend on leader age. *Journal of Organizational Behavior, 37*(8), 1224–1245. https://doi.org/10.1002/job.2101

Buengeler, C., Homan, A. C., & Voelpel, S. C. (2016b). The challenge of being a young manager: The effects of contingent reward and participative leadership on team-level turnover depend on leader age. *Journal of Organizational Behavior, 37*(8), 1224–1245. https://doi.org/10.1002/job.2101

Callahan, C., & Callahan, C. (2023, August 1). *Quiet quitters, snowflakes: Debunking generational stereotypes in the workplace*. WorkLife. https://www.worklife.news/culture/generational-mythbuster/

Collinson, C. (2023, October 17). *Best practices for engaging a multigenerational workforce*. Harvard Business Review. https://hbr.org/2023/10/best-practices-for-engaging-a-multigenerational-workforce#:~:text=Now%20and%20in%20the%20future,%2C%20productivity%2C%20and%20overall%20performance.

DePietro, A. (2018, August 14). *25 Best Business partner duos of all time*. GOBankingRates. https://www.gobankingrates.com/money/business/best-business-partner-duos-time/

Gallup, Inc. (2023, November 14). *Only a third of the oldest baby boomers in U.S. still working*. Gallup.com. http://www.gallup.com/poll/181292/third-oldest-baby-boomers-working.aspx

Glynn, P. (2023, December 11). *Retaining a multigenerational workforce (From baby boomers to Gen Z)*. Insight Global.

https://insightglobal.com/blog/retaining-multigenerational-workforce/

Helen Keller: "Alone we can do so little. Together we can do so much." (n.d.). The American Foundation for the Blind. https://www.afb.org/blog/entry/happy-birthday-helen

Magazine, C. (2023, July 3). Shaping Millennials to be the leaders of tomorrow. *The CEO Magazine.* https://www.theceomagazine.com/business/management-leadership/millennial-leaders/

Marousis, A. (2024, March 8). *What is the Ebbinghaus forgetting curve? Examples and strategies for overcoming it*. TalentCards. https://www.talentcards.com/blog/ebbinghaus-forgetting-curve/#:~:text=Identified%20by%20German%20psychologist%20Hermann,of%20what%20they've%20learned.

Pew Research Center. (2023, May 22). *Millennials are largest generation in the U.S. labor force.* http://www.pewresearch.org/fact-tank/2015/05/11/millennials-surpass-gen-xers-as-the-largest-generation-in-u-s-labor-force/

Pickup, O., & Anekola. (2023, July 29). *Gen Z workers are not tech-savvy in the workplace – and it's a growing problem.* WorkLife. https://www.worklife.news/technology/myth-buster-young-workers-are-not-tech-savvy-in-the-workplace-and-its-a-growing-problem/

Post, J. (2024, January 22). *What do millennials want in a modern leader?* business.com. https://www.business.com/articles/leadership-styles-millennials/

The Deloitte Global 2023 Gen Z and Millennial Survey. (2023, July 21). Deloitte. https://www.deloitte.com/global/en/issues/work/content/genzmillennialsurvey.html

The power of multigenerational teams in the social Sector (SSIR). (n.d.). (C) 2005-2024. https://ssir.org/articles/entry/the_power_of_multigenerational_teams_in_the_social_sector

This is What Leadership Looks Like in Each Generation. (n.d.). Skyline Group. https://skylineg.com/resources/blog/this-is-what-leadership-looks-like-in-each-generation

Usa, R., & Usa, R. (n.d.). *Randstad USA*. https://www.randstadusa.com/workforce360/managing-gen-y-z/

Made in United States
Troutdale, OR
01/17/2025